VAULT!

Every Gen Z's Guide to

Getting Through the Swamp of Adulting

JOHN LIM

Candid Creation Publishing

First published March 2023

Candid Creation Publishing books are available through most major bookstores in Singapore. For bulk order of our books at special quantity discounts, please email us at enquiry@ candidcreation.com.

VAULT!

EVERY GEN Z'S GUIDE TO GETTING THROUGH THE SWAMP OF ADULTING

Author   : John Lim
Publisher   : Phoon Kok Hwa
Editor   : Patricia Ng
Cover design   : Ryanne Ng
Layout   : Corrine Teng
Illustrator   : Meredith Poon
Published by   : Candid Creation Publishing LLP
                  167 Jalan Bukit Merah
                  #05-12 Connection One Tower 4
                  Singapore 150167
Website   : www.candidcreation.com
Facebook   : www.facebook.com/CandidCreationPublishing
Email   : enquiry@candidcreation.com

National Library Board, Singapore Cataloguing in Publication Data

Name(s): Lim, John, 1995-

Title: Vault! : every Gen Z's guide to getting through the swamp of adulting / John Lim.

Description: Singapore : Candid Creation Publishing, 2023. | Includes bibliography.

Identifier(s): ISBN 978-981-17258-8-3 (paperback)

Subject(s): LCSH: Adulthood. | Life skills.

Classification: DDC 646.700842--dc23

PRAISE FOR *VAULT!*

"There may be many different views on how the Gen Zs should tackle the future, but what we can all agree on is the hyper-complexity and uncertainty their future holds, and so kudos to John for trying to pen his thoughts to help the next generation, especially in Singapore!"

David Chua
CEO, National Youth Council

"The book is an attempt to provide helpful information to teens and early adults, popularly known as Generation Z, the Zoomers, regarding how to navigate the life of adulthood in more effective ways.

What is helpful about this book are the practical experiences offered by the author, given his own personal challenges with adult life, as well as documented experiences of others pointing to important lessons in life.

I strongly endorse this book to all potential readers of the Gen Z group, both for the teens and the early adults. For the former, it will be a helpful read to gain added skill in facing life's challenges; to the latter, its benefit is to have opportunity for reflection and evaluate how they may have fared in their own personal journey, the lessons from which could provide additional insight even as they become guides to those younger than them.

May you enjoy reading this worthwhile book in the quietness of your own heart. And please do not take for granted the insights suggested in its pages."

Valentino L Gonzales, PhD
MA-Licensed Professional Counsellor, State of Texas, USA

"There are many people who have struggled in their transition from school to work. But there is only ONE John who actually went through it, struggled through it, and came back to share his advice with you. John's *Vault!* is a rare find and count yourself lucky for grabbing this book. The distance that John went through to get all his stories and advice into a book just for you is truly extraordinary. I would highly recommend it to any schoolgoer regardless of where they are. If you want to succeed in this transition into the workforce and adulthood, *Vault!* is the book you would want to read."

Deddy Setiadi
Co-founder of Kodecoon Academy,
Author of *The A Student's Cheat Sheet*

"John has a genuine desire to help people holistically. His is a measured approach to life: not an absolute formula, but principles to be ingrained by experience. He speaks out of personal experience—having both thrived and struggled—as well as that of many others that he has included as examples in this book."

Caleb Chan
Young working adult and living enthusiast

"Whilst I may not fully understand the complexities of what Gen Zs face today, John's book is an essential read for this generation of Singaporeans confronting all the challenges and opportunities of a fast-changing world. Kudos to John for writing this book, as much for himself as for others like him!"

Christopher Gee
Senior Research Fellow, Institute of Policy Studies,
Lee Kuan Yew School of Public Policy

"This book DOES NOT try to sugar-coat. Every page in this book resonates and inspires. *Vault!* is a truly delightful book that offers unconventional yet practical insights into the realities of adulting, and shares how accepting failures in life helps to push us forward in our journey towards self-discovery. If you care deeply about managing the complexities of life and not letting circumstances get in the way of your dreams, this motivating book is a must-read for you."

Esther Reina
Songwriter

"Relatable examples that every 'job newbie' will go through. *Vault!* highlights possible experiences, questions, and even insights from various 'job veterans'. Take this as a guidebook to help you navigate different hurdles in your professional journey. Of course, like with every guidebook, you may not need to use all the information when you first receive the book. You'll go home to plan your next expedition, encountering similar or different experiences in the process. That's when you'll pick the guidebook up again."

Meredith Poon
The Gingerbread Pan

"As an entrepreneur, John's book deeply resonates with me. Running a fitness business today, I have seen how the emphasis on skill over passion and strength over weakness, have helped me to build a business, despite having never taken a business degree. I trust that John's book will continue to resonate for many young people, and highly recommend it to you."

Nicholas Ng
Fitness entrepreneur, @beachbodbrah

"I have known John for two years and seen him demonstrating wisdom and patience when going through challenges. Eager to listen and share about the way to deal with tough situations—in particular those that are work-related—with people from different backgrounds, ages, cultures, he also presents strong empathy with the younger generation. This book will be a useful read for everyone looking to make a helpful transition between school and work."

Stephanié Say, PhD
Research Scientist

"Moving from school life to real life afterward is indeed a critical point of everyone's life, especially in this world of full uncertainty. Explicitly, John can provocatively showcase the other side of real life that might be experienced especially by Gen Z who are not even being exposed to it. On the same pages, he balances it with recipes for Gen Z to start preparing and making the decision about their own future. It is no skip to read. Awesome work you have, John!"

Ari Yuda Laksmana, MM, ACC
Agile Leadership & Business Coach, Founder of Coaching Yuk, and CEO of Yumna Utama Kinerja (YUK) Corp

"I was really motivated by reading this. I am a sophomore in university majoring in environmental science and I also feel conscious about my journey. I could get many tips to help me make my decision for the future by reading this. If you are struggling with something with your pathway and what you should do now, this book will be helpful for you to make a decision."

Koharu Alicia Senda
Student, Osaka Prefecture University

To you, the Gen Z,
may the *fight* be in you.

CONTENTS

FOREWORD

I first met John in 2018 when I joined the University of Nottingham Students' Union (UoNSU) as their Chief Executive. He was a Student Trustee—a current student who volunteered, along with various others to make up the Board of Trustees whose collective role was to lead and govern UoNSU, an independent charity representing the interests of and providing developmental and community opportunities for some 35,000 students.

John was a curious character. Relentlessly positive, John was keen to learn as well as to contribute, and had possession of a brain that worked like no other I had encountered. He was proactive, and sought out conversations with me, keen to understand my intended approach in my early days at UoNSU whilst gently, yet assertively applying his own steerage. I really enjoyed my time working with John.

John always had a whiteboard marker in hand, and it never took much for him to spring from his chair to scribble musingly, creatively, intelligently, conjuring pathways, analogies and pictographic representations articulating the challenge, the opportunity and almost always, the solution, to the matter being pondered. I loved it when I saw the twinkle in John's eye opposite me at the boardroom table; I knew we were about to be entertained and excited as he weaved his marker productively through the problem to the prize.

I've never yet come across a Trustee, nor indeed a person, quite like John. I found him inquisitive, supportive, challenging, inspirational, in a way no other had before or has since. On occasion, I find myself reminiscing of my time working with John, his influence still within reach when I need a helping hand to spike my own analysis of a situation. How might John look at this? Where would his whiteboard marker take us?

In this book, I can see quite vividly how John has applied his critical thinking to the challenges of early adult life. In fact, I can see him scribbling on the whiteboard, hear him describing his thought processes, and I find myself grinning with enthusiasm at the unique solutions he has arrived at.

I'm particularly pleased to see the prominence that John places on the role of values—the express articulation of the character of an individual or organisation. It's so important to assess one's "fit" with an organisation. Make a wrong choice and it just won't work. Take the time to investigate what matters most to you and find the people, the direction, the type of contribution you wish to make in the world, and all else will fall in line behind those decisions. That's why I work in students' unions; because I love coming across and supporting future leaders like John who wish to make a positive contribution in service of others, and it pleases me greatly to see his contribution playing through this book.

John has clearly been through a lot and has applied his wonderfully analytical brain to the examination of his own journey to and through adulthood. The result is something both aspirational and practical which is designed to help others to do as he has done— to find serenity coupled with a fulfilling productivity. I wish him and you well in your respective life journeys.

Daryl Omerod
Chief Executive,
Sheffield Students' Union

PREFACE

THE STORY BEHIND THIS BOOK

I'm in a clinic. There's a stack of *National Geographic* magazines in the corner. The receptionist sits behind the counter, sullen-faced, scribbling. In the clinic, everyone is silent. There's no laughter or chatter. People are either looking at their phones or at the doctor's door, waiting for the doctor to call them.

It's a strange place. Here, the doctor comes out to call you, with a smile on his face.

Maybe it's because it's a psychiatrist's clinic.

You didn't read that wrong. I'm in a psychiatrist's clinic. It's not a place I ever expected to find myself in after graduating.

You see the happy faces of graduates, throwing their mortar boards, writing testimonials about how university was the best time of their lives, with prestigious job titles under their names—Doctor, Lawyer, Investment Banker … and you think that's going to be your experience.

It wasn't mine.

After graduating, I struggled to find a job in Singapore. I didn't expect this after graduating with a first-class honours degree, with work experiences in China, Peru, and the UK, and former experiences as a board director.

One moment you're talking with directors and senior executives, and the next moment, you're struggling to even get the HR assistant to answer your call.

Oh, the irony.

The anxiety of finding a job led me to use food as a coping mechanism. I stuffed my face with food to distract myself from the anxiety of sending in job applications. I would gobble down cakes, cookies, and chocolates, often tearing through an entire box of the last, not stopping even when I felt full.

Within a month, I gained 8 kilogrammes.

Searching for a job can feel like a hopeless process. You don't know what you're looking for. If you've been job hunting for some time, desperation sets in. When you first graduate, you probably had a dream job. But after constant rejections, you learn to settle for less. Drop your hopes. Go for something less.

But even then, you still get rejection after rejection.

The worst thing? You have parents who are pressuring you to get a job.

University, school told you all the nice things about what life would be like after school. They publish graduate earnings and showcase former alumni who have gotten into famous companies.

Oh, and they remember to call you to donate.

Reality is much more sombre. What makes it worse is that there's little support after school to help you through that journey. Your friends have moved onto different paths in life. Your parents were born in a different generation.

It can feel lonely. Desperate. Hopeless.

WHY THIS BOOK WAS WRITTEN

That's why this book was written. Because the transition between school and work is complex. It's a wicked problem that's not easily encompassed in the tidy narrative that society presents us:

school → work → partner → family → retirement

Instead, it's more like a tumble dryer, where phases are mixed up, rarely coming one after another, and sometimes even repeating.

This book was written so you don't feel alone in your journey.

Think of it as a heart-warming mug of hot chocolate on a cold, rainy day. When you want to give up, throw in the towel, and resign to life. You know that feeling—of not wanting to fight anymore. When your sigh is not a sigh of relief.

It's a sigh of *resignation*.

It *says,* "I give up. I don't want to do this anymore. Why does no one believe in me? Why does no one give me a chance?"

I wish you hope through this book. Each time you open this book, I pray it gives you strength to carry on for another day. Because you don't have to know the whole way. You only need to have enough for *this* day.

Don't think of it as a workbook. Think of it as a *walkbook*— where you paste, doodle, and jot down your thoughts in the book.

Writing this book, I wanted answers to questions such as:

- How do you find what you're good at?
- How do you find a job?
- How do you get your colleagues to like you?
- How do you succeed at your job?

In my first temporary role, I was sacked from Google. I then performed so badly in my first full-time job that I was issued with a Performance Improvement Plan (a get-better-or-get-sacked plan).

This is not the normal experience for most people. I don't want you to be in that position. But somehow, some of us seem to land up in positions where we may not like our jobs or the people we work with, and/or struggle to understand why we never seem to get promoted, no matter how hard we try.

A friend of mine from university, Ariel (not her real name) was awarded a scholarship to study overseas, a clear sign of her academic ability from a young age. She moved to the UK when she was only 16.

Yet in her first year at work, she faced so much difficulty that she actively thought about ending her life.

Why? It's a question whose answers have eluded me. If academic ability is no indication of one's ability to transit into adulthood and the workplace effectively, then what is? What can help someone to flourish better during this transition? What are the principles?

Why do some people thrive in their jobs, whilst others struggle so badly?

In this book, I first share principles that have worked for people. There are no quick hacks. Only first principles, which would work whether we were in 2022. Or 2202.

Secondly, this book reflects the true ups *and downs* of careers. Often, we see the ups, where there are the tidy 10 tips to acing your interview! Or 5 principles to get your dream job! This book offers idealism, but also balances it with a dose of reality. Included are the real life struggles of others who have faced difficulties at their jobs.

Look at the shelves of career advice books, and you will find many who share how they have climbed in their career. Kudos to them, but the real world of work is not so tidy. It's built on the backs of people who struggle to make ends meet, who get scolded by bosses, and miss out on promotions.

The career story of Cath (not her real name) is the most inspirational I've heard. Cath is a single mother with two teenage children. When I visit her at home, we would often sit on the floor, because they couldn't afford a dining table.

Once, she shared what her daughter told her: "You know, sometimes I'm shy of you because my friends' mothers work in offices. But you only work at KFC."

As she shares this, tears roll down her face. "All I want to do is to provide for them. Everything I earn, I give them."

Cath's career may not necessarily be big, heroic, or famous, but these are the jobs that contribute something to the things or the people you love.

These are the real stories of careers. Not a rapid ascent up the career ladder, but hardscrabble jobs, where people fight to make a living.

Careers are a call to adventure. They are the start of a hero's journey. Your hero's journey. When you work at something that has meaning for you, you are walking into a journey where you will fight, tooth and nail, to get to where you want to be.

HOW THIS BOOK IS STRUCTURED

There are largely two types of books: those that offer ideas, and those that offer implementation.

Those that offer ideas tell you about concepts, but have little practical application. Those that offer implementation focus on how you can apply the advice to your unique situation.

This book balances ideas and implementation. Whilst I do offer some ideas, I believe that real change comes when you take action. Having worked with thousands of students, I've found that the best way is for you to be inspired by an idea, implement it, and constantly iterate it for your own life.

This book builds on the employee life cycle model, a common framework for employers or Human Resource (HR) professionals to determine different actions at varying points in an employee's time in the company. It was chosen because most employees would pass through the six stages. But in this book, the model used turns the focus on you, the employee, rather than the employer.

It layers the Employee Life Cycle model (Fig. P.1) with the Emotion Life Cycle (Fig. P.2), a model I created to help you better understand the emotions you face throughout key transitory stages at work. Beyond giving you a framework to understand what you're facing, it also brings tools to aid in your transition.

Fig. P.1 The six key stages of the Employee Life Cycle model.

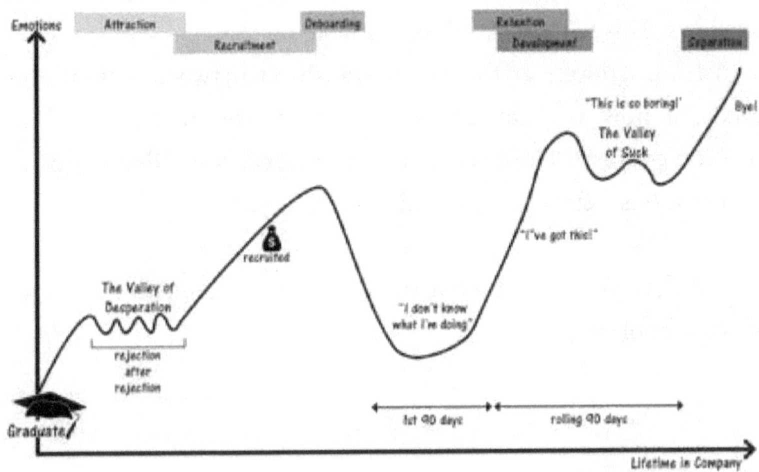

Fig. P.2 The Emotion Life Cycle:
Emotions against a lifetime in a company.

Each chapter looks at the common advice we hear from society at each career stage. I then ask questions such as:

- Does this advice still work?
- Is it still relevant?

Each chapter contains interviews with people who've struggled in that particular stage of work, and also others who have successfully overcome that stage.

To help you implement, each section has an ACT portion, filled with simple actions you can do to make changes you want to see.

THIS BOOK IS NOT FOR EVERYONE

This book is *not* for you if you want advice on cover letters, CVs, and interviews. This will not teach you how to do that.

Instead, it looks at the wider transition between school and work, and how you can thrive in that transition. Because that transition comprises more than just your career, we will also look at your emotions, relationships, and outlook on life.

So before we look at what thriving at work looks like, let's go back to school.

1

THE SCHOOL OF ADULTING

WHY A SCHOOL OF ADULTING?

What is adulting anyway? The Oxford dictionary defines this as "the practice of behaving in a way characteristic of a responsible adult, especially the accomplishment of mundane but necessary tasks". In the context of this book, I would define adulting as "transiting between school and adulthood".

It's a two-way transition that involves a constant moving back and forth between adulthood and school. Here, adulthood refers to the multiple stages that are encompassed within your early years when you become an adult, such as, getting your first full-time job, getting married, and buying a home.

Secondly, don't think of school as a physical place, but more as a state of mind. It's where you go to learn. There are times when you will struggle as an adult. During those times, humble yourself to learn what you need to move forward. It may not necessarily be through a classroom, but can be through learning from mentors, or experimenting.

This transition between school and adulthood covers four different areas:

- Work
  - » How do I succeed in my job?
  - » How do I get promoted?

- Wealth
  - » How do I plan my finances?
  - » How should I grow my wealth?
  - » How should I preserve my wealth?
- Health
  - » How do I stay fit when I'm so busy?
- Happiness
  - » How do I make friends?

If you think about it, it's not fair, is it? You had professors at university. Teachers at school. Mummy accompanied you to kindergarten. But when you move into adulthood, because you have a school leaving certificate, you're expected to know it all.

As author Scott Peck once said, "Life *is* difficult." It is! Having better handles would help.

Let's first start with why adulting is so difficult.

You Forget the Most Important Lesson

The complexities and change of life on Earth mean that we are put in situations which demand emotional dexterity and nuance. It's no longer about rules for what you do in each situation.

But it becomes a *weighing* of the different rules, and balance amongst the different things you know. That's why adulting is a skill that *must* be learnt. Just as the professional footballer doesn't kick every single ball that comes to him the same way, the *professional* adult doesn't treat every single situation the same way. As former US President Barack Obama said in Michael Lewis' *Vanity Fair* article "Obama's Way":

"You wind up dealing with probabilities. Any given decision you make you will wind up with a 30 to 40 percent chance that it isn't going to work. You have to own that and feel comfortable with the way you made the decision."

The most important lesson in school we may have missed is that of *balance*. It's the ability to weigh probabilities and decide based on that. Remember your math class on statistics? There's no definite, 100% guaranteed, decision. Only the percentage probability of an event's occurrence.

We are dealing with decisions that have a *lead-up*, and also what I call a *lead-down*.

The lead-up refers to the ability to analyse and think through the decision you are making. This involves an understanding of probabilities.

One mental tool that helps is the outcome projection tool, introduced by Shane Melaugh, the co-founder of Thrive Themes, the WordPress plug-in software.

On a scale, map out the different outcomes that may happen. On one end, write down the best case scenario. On the other end, write down the worst case scenario. In the middle, write down an "average case" scenario. Then go out to find the probabilities of that happening.

The lead-down refers to how you execute on the decision that you've made.

In Lee Freeman-Shor's book, *The Art of Execution*, he studied 1,866 investments made by famous investors. What shocked him was this.

He found that only 49% of the ideas made money. On average, their ideas were wrong! Yet despite this, these investors almost *never* lost money.

That prompted him to ask: How are they making lots of money if their ideas are wrong most of the time?

He found that successful stock market investing was not about being right. Instead, *success in investing is down to how great ideas are executed.*

It was what they did *after* they made the decision, rather than what happened *before* the decision.

Similarly, in your decision-making, it's ensuring that the thinking that leads *up* to the decision is robust. But how you execute in the lead *down*, after the decision made is equally crucial.

Your *implementation* counts as much as the initial decision. Often, we can analyse the benefits of a particular career decision. But it's how we execute on that decision that reaps us its benefits.

When you make a career decision that doesn't work out, have the guts to say, "I don't think this is working out", and adjust. It's not trying to stick to something that's hopeless. It's learning to *quit.*

Quitting sounds taboo. We hear about gritting our teeth, but not enough about *giving up.* Sometimes, we make bad decisions where quitting is the only saving grace. But the sunk-cost fallacy— where we continue sticking with commitments because of our prior emotional investment—can sometimes keep us stuck.

When you're faced with the reality that something is not working or will not work out, accepting reality moves you forward.

In 2015, my life nearly tipped over the edge. In the lead up to Christmas, whilst festive cheer filled the streets, and shoppers ploughed the stores for Christmas presents, my mind was filled with emotional distress.

Each day, I would take a chair to the fourteenth storey of my apartment block, stand on it, and wonder if I should tip myself over. I was devastated. I didn't know what to do with my life.

I didn't know the point of continuing on with life.

Why?

Faced with the reality that I could not get into medical school, I could not accept it. I wanted to quit this game called life. It made me realise how unprepared I was for life.

You're Not Prepared

It's funny how growing up, we were taught more about math (managed to use integration in your life yet?) than about our *mind*.

That's why this book, beyond focusing on the practical actions you can take to thrive as a Gen Z in the workplace, also looks at equipping you with the *mental* tools for doing better in this game called life.

Make no mistake. Without the mental and emotional fitness to deal with the curveballs that life throws at you, you may find yourself lonely, languishing, and lost. Yes, we might have that starry-eyed approach to life, saying Instagrammable quotes like, "Not all who wander are lost".

But you and I know that the times when we are lost, are the times when we have no desire to continue any longer.

We may try finding another self-help book. The biggest myth these "self-development" books have (please don't call me a nerd for having read thousands!), is the assumption that you are the problem. You need to work harder. You need to be more Y. You need to buy Z.

But we often don't take a step back and think: How if it wasn't our fault? What if we simply weren't taught the skills to flourishing in life?

That's why the premise of this book is:

Adulting is a skill that can be learnt,
with an emphasis on relationship, rather than experience.

- **Adulting is a skill that can be learnt**
Why is adulting a skill? Look around you.

You see some friends who are succeeding as adults, who are tenacious and resilient, despite the situations they are in. Others are struggling. What differentiates the adults who thrive, and those who don't? I once asked Sascha, currently a Vice President at Siemens ASEAN, about how he got so far in his career.

"I guess I was lucky," was his reply.

Yes, there may be an element of luck.

But as the saying goes, "Fortune favours the bold". Those who find themselves lucky, find themselves prepared to seize the opportunity when luck shines down on them.

What I've found is that many of these thriving adults see adulting as a *skill*.

We may not think of adulting as a skill. We think of it more as something that comes to us over time. Yet this isn't an approach that works. Doing that reduces your intentionality about how you become a better adult. You weren't born knowing how to manage your finances, or how to present to your bosses. You learnt those skills and applied them.

Why not take the same approach of intention towards growing your adulting skill?

- **Through a focus on relationships, rather than experiences**
Our world today is built on experiences.

Apps strive for the best user experience that is smooth, intuitive, and user-friendly.

Companies deliver customer experiences that address our wants, immediately. It's no longer enough for Amazon Prime. It needs to be Amazon Prime *Now*. Google recommends us search results *before* we've even typed them. We seek the best food, holidays, and items that will satisfy the desires within us.

As we transit to adulthood, we may focus more on the *experiences* we have than the relationships within yourself, and with others. We may embrace adulting for the freedoms it brings, such as the first full-time salary that allows you to buy anything you want, without asking your parents.

But we forget that experiences like the excitement you have upon receiving a phone for the first time will end. Relationships, though, last for longer. They help you to persist through the difficulties of adulting and support you along your journey.

It is relationships that matter, not experiences. To thrive as a young adult, build a tapestry of relationships under you that enable you to bounce back whenever you fall, and pulls you out of your comfort zone to reach even further in your life.

To start on our adulting journey, we need to start from within, rather than looking outwards. It's about finding *yourself*, before you even find a job.

It starts with the story of Deddy.

DON'T LOSE YOURSELF: DEDDY'S STORY

I'm arranging to meet Deddy, the co-founder of Kodecoon, a coding school for students. He asks if we should have dinner together.

I tell him the truth. As a young person struggling to finance this book and my business, I need to save every dollar I can. I ask him if he minds me bringing my dinner from home. Immediately, he replies, "Hey John, I buy you dinner. *Lai*, my treat." (*Lai* is Chinese for "come".)

It's a tremendous gesture of generosity, especially when we haven't physically met before.

Ever since I met him, I've been interested in his story because of how invested he is in teaching the future generation. I ask about advice he has for young adults for better adulting.

Deddy's first advice is to fail fast, and fail often. He starts with the myths that society inculcates in our young people.

"Mistakes. A lot of people are very afraid of making mistakes," he says.

He shares how in the past, his "hobby" was going to Popular Bookstore to try assessment papers. If he didn't make any mistakes, he wouldn't buy the book. It shows his desire to want to be wrong. To prove that he could be wrong.

"I came up with the Dead Fish List for my students to hang it on the wall. A list of your failures. If you don't have failures, you don't learn.

"Walls are there to be 'banged'. If you think it can't work, just try. And 'boom!' And I realise that when you knock against it, it may not be a wall. Maybe it's a revolving door. Open it, and a door leads to another door. The more walls you knock, the more you go next time 'Ah, I know this is a wall, so I don't bang it.'"

The second crucial adulting skill is decision-making. What does he recommend to young people to help them decide better?

He replies, "Build life after school. Don't just study."

When he was 15, he was given an opportunity to teach a 14-year-old social studies. He told his older brother that he didn't know how. But his brother encouraged him to give it a go.

"Many are stuck because they are scared of uncertainty. Then reduce the uncertainty! That's why I went to do nine internships! I wanted to know what was in the different industries."

Even though Deddy is an accomplished business owner today, his decision-making skills weren't as polished initially.

His own career story reads like a drama. When he was fresh out of university, he was offered a role as an investment banker.

He turned it down. Deddy didn't think he could live the life of an investment banker, hosting clients, making rich people richer.

Then he went into the finance department of a multinational company. There, he was selected to go to the US, where he was given his own apartment, his own car, and he thought, "Wow, this is the life."

But at that time, he was already running Kodecoon, the coding school for students. One day, his boss found out. His boss had been looking for some coding classes for his son. His boss wrote him an email, inviting him to "coffee".

During the grilling, his boss showed him Kodecoon on his computer. Deddy turned the tables around. He asked his boss, "If you take off your boss hat, and put on the hat of a father, what would you advise me?"

The boss looks at Deddy. Then at the screen with Kodecoon's Facebook page. This went on for a minute.

"Don't quote me. Go all in."

His boss points at the computer. With Kodecoon on it.

The irony? His boss sent both children to Deddy's classes.

Still, Deddy didn't quit his job. He even wanted to quit his business. It was only a few months later, when he asked himself, "Will I regret this in two years' time, if I didn't do this?"

His advice for decision-making is simple: *Always go back to the heart.*

But what if this "heart" thing is very different from what society says is "right"? What if a young person might want to be a busker, when the conventional path would be to enter banking? How do we encourage them to *be* different? And to follow that difference?

"Tough question. You need to believe. Because if I stopped believing in the things I'm hearing inside, it's dead. The biggest naysayer is you.

"You are the protector of the flame. Sometimes it might take longer than you think it should be. You might go broke. You don't wait for the stars and dream, and not do anything about it. If you want to protect this flame, do something. Build a wall around it.

"Go and learn. Meet people. Talk to people. Knock on doors.

"My advice to the young ones who have this little flame that is different, protect it. There will be people who try to blow this out. Even your own parents. Theirs is the biggest blow.

"You need to know that you're ultimately the protector."

For adults choosing between heart and the hard realities of making a living, Deddy's advice bears relevance. It's about deciding, and going all out to make it happen.

But how does one deal with the uncertainty of the decisions they make as adults?

"Reduce what you don't know. Go and experience new things," he advises.

Deddy shares an experience he had in high school, where he saw his friends taking SATs, applying to UK and US universities. His first thought?

"Eh *bojio*?" (*Bojio* is a Singlish slang for "why didn't you invite me?")

It made him realise the future value of letting his children see "famous" schools like Harvard. He wants his children to know, "It's just a building. The professor doesn't eat rocks. They eat rice. They eat bread."

I laugh.

"When we are young, we have this psychological barrier. But the moment you see others do it, you say, 'I can do this as well.' When you say that, whatever you dream, you can see. It becomes real.

"When I did a survey with my students, 90% of my students struggled with procrastination. What works for me is to decide. You procrastinate because you don't make the decision.

"You procrastinate about whether you should revise now or next week.

"We are stuck because we don't decide. If you decided that you want to do well, there's no need to procrastinate. There's no dilemma."

For adults vacillating in their decisions, Deddy offers a clear way. Decide, and commit. Once you decide, don't look back. Go all out to make what you want happen.

But I wonder what Deddy's biggest takeaway from his journey is.

"It's always the valleys in my life that have taught me the biggest lessons. Super cliche. But it's those things that give you the opportunity to fail, to be different, to think differently, to be a misfit. That becomes your deepest strength.

"The world has so much of these mediocre people. People who try to follow others. Until they lose themselves.

"Don't lose your own identity."

As you transit to adulthood, there are expectations and obligations that will be placed upon you. Expectations of when you will marry, or the obligation to support your parents. But Deddy's advice on adulting is different from the common narrative of taking the tried and tested route. Instead, he encourages you to dream, decide, and commit. To protect the flame within you, allowing no one to blow it out.

Growing up, you had certain dreams and hopes of how you would want your career to be. Society or your closest family may have blown out that flame. Finding that flame again requires you to rebuild a relationship with *yourself*, knowing yourself, tuning into the crackle of the flame within you.

Knowing yourself is knowing four different elements of who you are—your story, your values, your strengths, and your personality—framed within the wider context of the future of work (Fig. 1.1, overleaf).

Fig. 1.1 A framework for knowing yourself better.

KNOW YOUR STORY

We all have a story. But the question is: Whose story are you living?

As a young adult, you will be fed stories by society about how a "proper" adult should behave.

In Singapore, there's a common narrative.

1. Graduate…
2. Get a job…
3. Constantly upgrade yourself by going for courses…
4. Get married…
5. Have babies…

It's a tidy narrative of progress and upward mobility. But as an adult, this may not be the narrative you believe in, or want. It may also not be the way you see your own story play out.

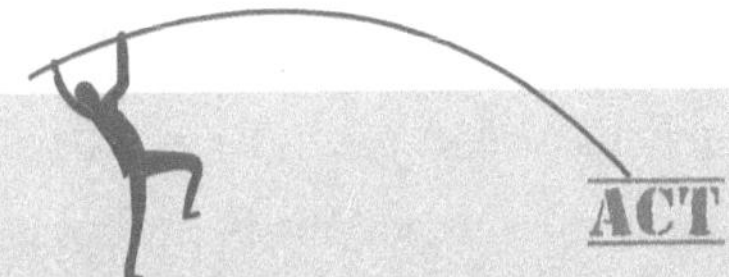

The Life Story Exercise

On a piece of paper, take time to plot out significant events in your life. Look back at the course of your life and ask:

1. What is your history? What were significant turning point moments in your life?
2. What did you learn at those points?
3. What is your story now?
4. What is the future story you want to write?

This exercise shows you what you've overcome, and the lessons from those moments. As you look back, these turning-point moments will inform the future story you want to write. Did you give up on certain dreams because your parents advised you to "be realistic"?

Before thriving as a young adult, *think* of what your own narrative is. Many of us live without thinking about how the cultural lenses we put on may shape our approach to life. Our loved ones and our environment play a significant role in influencing what we want. They will tell you that X, Y, and Z are important.

But what is your story? What is meaningful to you?

Crafting our own meaningful stories requires us to know our values.

KNOW YOUR VALUES

Do you know your values? Much has been said about values, and how important they are. But *knowing* your values is different from living them out. Let's say you prided integrity. What happens if you see your friend being dishonest? Would you report him to the authorities?

Values can serve as anchors in our lives. But these anchors are also *retractable*. When we are put in situations where our values are in conflict, we are forced to assess what our wider desired outcomes are.

These value anchors can then be retracted. They are not black and white determinants of action. Rather they serve to *guide* your action. The key is to know what your baseline values are, and when you're making an exception for them.

KNOW YOUR PERSONALITY

Ariel (who you were introduced to in the Preface) admits. For years, she pretended that she loved being around people. When she was around people, she would laugh, make jokes, and look very interested in their stories. But inside, she felt like she was dying.

It was not until she fully owned her personality as an introvert that she intentionally searched for smaller teams to work with. This eventually earned her a promotion! Knowing your personality is important in understanding what will best fit you in the world of work.

How do you find out your personality?

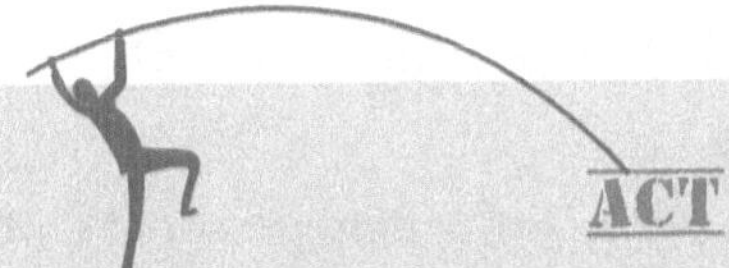

Take the MBTI Test

The Myers-Briggs Type Indicator (MBTI) is a tool to help individuals identify their own personality types so that they can better understand their communication preference and the way they interact with others as well as how they perceive the world and make decisions. You can find out more at:

https://www.myersbriggs.org/

But John, isn't this a fixed mindset? If the personality test says we are weak at something, shouldn't we try our best to improve it? Isn't that the growth mindset?

Yes and no.

Whilst not accepting your current performance level is vital, improving your performance at things your personality is not well suited for may not yield the greatest fruits. In his classic article "Managing Oneself", management guru Peter Drucker explains that it takes far more effort to improve from an area of incompetence to mediocrity than it is to improve from good to great performance.

He argues that executives have to understand their personality. They should ask themselves whether they work best with people, or as a loner. "If you then work well with people, you then must ask, 'In what relationship?'" He points out the example of General George S. Patton, whom the US Chief of Staff George Marshall observed would be the "the best subordinate ... but the worst commander."

The most effective people work with their personality, rather than against it. Being fixated on work that fits with your personality and systematically growing your skill at that makes the difference between you and a mediocre worker.

KNOW YOUR STRENGTH

One myth you often hear is that it's better to improve your weaknesses, and be well-rounded. That's not necessarily true. Working from your strengths ensures that you're *compounding* your competitive advantage over someone else, over time.

Your skills are unique to you. What comes naturally to you doesn't come naturally to someone else. Focusing on them will bring you the greatest return on your investment, rather than desperately trying to improve your weaknesses.

It's tempting to focus on your weaknesses because you quickly see a sharp rise in your ability at it. When you hone your strength, despite working hard at it, you may not see any change. That can be frustrating, especially when you wonder if what you do is having any effect on what you're doing. There's no seeming feedback for the effort you're putting in.

Naval Ravikant, the angel investor who invested in the likes of Uber and is today the co-founder of AngelList, shares the example of how a good software engineer, simply by writing the right piece of code, can create half a billion dollars' worth of value. But ten engineers working ten times as hard may have wasted their time because of certain wrong decisions regarding the code they built.

"You want to get into a leveraged job where you control your own time and you're tracked on the outputs. If you do something incredible to move the needle on the business, they have to pay you. Especially if they don't know how you did it because it's innate to your obsession or your skill."

Improving your weaknesses may only make you mediocre in them and may not make that much of a difference in your work compared to others. As management professor Morten Hansen found in his study of 5,000 executives, the most effective ones were those who focused on their strengths and systematically said "no" to their weaknesses.

Focusing on your skill, rather than your weakness, will bring you exponential returns, rather than the linear returns of a focus on your weaknesses.

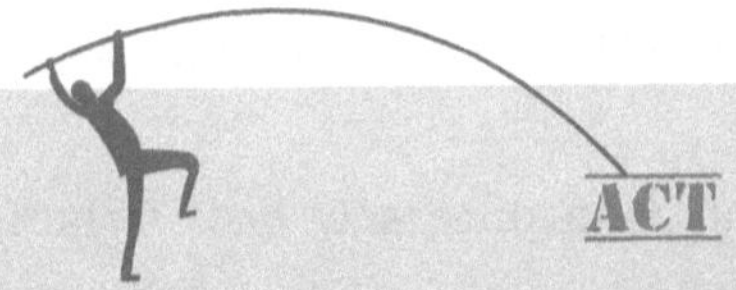

Take the CliftonStrengths test by Gallup.

Formerly known as the Clifton StrengthsFinder assessment, this is a test that helps individuals discover their top five strengths and the intensity of these talents. You can find out more here:

https://www.gallup.com/cliftonstrengths/en/252137/home.aspx

After taking the test, ask yourself these questions.

1. Do you find it an accurate description of your strengths?
2. What doesn't seem to be an accurate description? Why?
3. What is the smallest action you are going to take to apply those strengths?

KNOW THE FUTURE OF WORK: CHRIS'S ADVICE

Christopher Gee is a Gen X senior researcher at a Singaporean think tank. As a researcher, he's particularly interested in how generations transfer wealth.

We begin with Chris's observations about the workplace today. His first observation is about technology. He observes how technology has changed the face of work, allowing people to work anywhere, anytime.

But he argues that technology has made work increasingly precarious, with technology exposing traditionally insulated industries to global market forces.

"Many employers today are built around an industrial model of labour. It's like a factory. Even a university hires people on an almost industrial type basis. I hire the lecturer to teach. And they have certain KPIs or teaching hours to keep to."

Then he asks me, "When you were at university, did you experience strikes?"

I laugh. As a Singaporean who once saw how strikes were severely punished, my first experience of strikes at Nottingham was a curious experience. Daily, I would see lecturers stand by the university entrance, raising placards, whilst drivers passing would honk in support.

Chris observed how his eldest, studying in the UK, had lessons which were disrupted by strikes by the lecturers.

"The universities are moving away from that industrial model to a more flexible model of zero hours contracts. More and more teaching staff being forced to have these zero hours contracts, are rebelling.

"The game has suddenly changed. 'My life is precarious. I have an advanced degree, or even a PhD. But I'm being subjected to working conditions that are essentially no different to a food deliveryman.'"

It bears noting that the traditional model of credentials equating to employment is now breaking down. It means that your parents' advice on studying hard to get a good job may not always be true.

"Why? Because the teaching model has also broken down," says Chris. "Why do I want to spend that much time learning all of that very specialised instruction, when it could be completely obsolete? By the time I graduate, the stuff I'm being taught, is most likely obsolete. They've been taught by lecturers that may have zero practical experience.

"The world is changing so fast.

"One needs to be a lot more regular with learning. We can't be concentrating on it so much, in the first 12 to 15 years of your life. Now, it's even longer—20 years. Once you pass kindergarten, you get into this very intensive, singular track education system that leads you to a degree. It's very lumpy. That investment is very intense initially.

"There's a big jump in education expenses, when you're between 12 and 25 in Singapore. It then falls off after that, because you finish your undergrad studies. That's very concentrated and upfront. It's all spent on acquiring an education and ending up in a world that is hugely different."

He points to my own example. I committed to this degree, at great expense, with no good outcome. It was a big, concentrated, and a very *bad* bet.

Chris's advice for Gen Zs?

"Take smaller bets and be more flexible and adaptable. Customise the learning to the interest and the specific purpose and impact, that is designed by each individual."

Adulting better may thus be about taking smaller bets over a life course, rather than concentrated bets.

This is where you see the wisdom of people like Facebook employee, Chen Jun, who credited micro-courses to landing his current role. These micro-courses target a specific gap you see in your inability to do something and move you to a point where you *can* do it well.

Chris goes a step further.

"Everything is a learning opportunity. The delivery rider going up the hill, can learn something. If all they're doing and thinking is "Oh, my God, what a hard ride it is up this hill!" they've probably not learnt very much.

"You should capture all of this and use as much of it in your CV. That's how you customise all of these individual learning experiences.

"You may say, 'Okay, I was a delivery rider for three years. But this is what I learnt for myself, about the world. And this is what this learning helps me in telling you where I'm going to deliver value to you.'

"And that future employer may be you, yourself, because you've learnt all of these things. Instead of riding a bike and delivering food, you now know what you can do, in other areas."

His last piece of advice?

"You craft your own job description. Expecting a job description is like expecting a model answer. You are the employer. No one will know you, your skills, better than you do. You need to know your value and what's the value you bring that will drive that job description. The job description is for you to make."

Chris's advice on crafting your own job description forces us to think about how we should no longer work expecting work to be told to us. Instead, transiting into adulthood, we must first think about where we can best add value to any organisation. It's knowing your strengths.

Then, it's customising where you add best to work that would truly drive value within the organisation.

Lastly, it's learning in a regular, customised manner, so that you cover up the gaps you see in your ability.

Chris's interview may have filled you with some anxieties. If even people with PhDs were not assured of jobs, how can *you* be certain of job security?

To adult better in this different world of work requires us to understand two shifts in the world of work.

Here's a question. What differentiates you, the *full-time* employee, working from home, from a *freelancer* today? The freelancer has many different gigs, for many different clients who pay him, but no single employer. He is his own employer. He is untethered to any employer, and therefore has the flexibility to determine his own work. Doesn't that sound like you, even if you have a full-time job today, as you work from home?

You have many different work products to work on. You are delivering work remotely. You can work anywhere, anytime. You can even take on other remote jobs if you wanted to.

This accelerating trend from office-bound work to work-from-home has opened up possibilities for employers. There are two key shifts.

Firstly, as Jay Ng, the CEO of Weshine, an employment platform based in Indonesia, noted: the entry level computer engineer can be hired remotely today. There is no longer a need for employers to keep to their geographical location in sourcing for cheaper talent. You're no longer competing locally, but globally. If you're asking for the median salary where you're based, and someone in a less-developed nation requires much less, what differentiates you from that cheaper talent?

But that's not new. With the digital revolution, companies were increasingly able to source for global, cheaper talent that could plug in from anywhere in the world.

What's new is the second shift. It's the shift from full-time work, to *just-in-time* work. Covid-19 forced companies to "right-size" (a nicer phrase to describe retrenchments) their operations. A permanent workforce may not seem the best value for money. Instead, you can get just-in-time work, where you deal directly with a freelancer for a specific work product, rather than hiring someone as a permanent fixture. Rather than having *permanent* staff, there may be a shift towards more *performance* artists, who come in to perform a set task.

In their paper studying the marginalisation of graduate freelancers in the gig economy, Reuben Ng and Paul Wong observed how employers are now paying per task, rather than per unit *time*.

The proliferation of platform work on the likes of Upwork or Grab is a clear example. These platform workers are paid per task, rather than by time. They are offered protections insofar as they work, so that they can return to work. Much of the benefits (such as healthcare) are premised on the worker getting back to work for the platform, rather than building up the worker's future capital. Retirement benefits like pensions are not included. Workers are trading their time for money, but with none of the long-term benefits such as pensions, retirement, and career development.

To cope with the changing face of work, you don't want to be the instrument of labour, but owning the instrument of labour. Philosopher Karl Marx's words in *Das Kapital* in 1867 seem an uncanny description of what work is like today as a full-time employee.

"'When he was seven years old I used to carry him to work on my back to and fro through the snow, and he used to work 16 hours a day. ... I have often knelt down to feed him, as he stood by the machine, for he could not leave it or stop.'

Fed meals as he worked, as a steam engine is fed coal and water, this child was 'an instrument of labour.'"

Beholden to the employer, who provides all of our needs, we may sometimes find ourselves becoming "dispensable" when the company no longer finds a need for our services. That's when we are retrenched.

That's why we need a different construct for the new world of work.

THE T-SHAPED GEN Z

What I really want to say is this. If you're a young employee today, a Gen Z who's recently started work, you're screwed.

School or university has corralled you into a tidy niche with a degree, imparting you with knowledge or skills in that specific domain. That may limit your ability to constantly reinvent yourself for a different industry. That's why this book focuses so much on the following construct.

The T-Shaped Gen Z. It is adapted from the British notion of the T-shaped designer. As Professor Alex Milton said of the T-shaped designer:

"There is a notion in Britain of a T-shaped designer, one with depth of discipline in a single area but also a breadth of empathy for other areas of design."

Jony Ive, the former Chief Design Officer of Apple who designed the Mac, iPod, and iPhone, was trained in industrial design at Newcastle Polytechnic (now known as Northumbria University). He had a broad design education that exposed him to fine artists, fashion designers, and graphic designers.

But at the same time, Ive had the chance to immerse himself in hands-on design, making and prototyping designs he had in mind with a project-based education. It was furthered by the "double-sandwich course structure", where the first year was followed by two years of placements in industry, before ending in a last year at university. These placements allowed students to bridge theory and application. It gave Ive the depth in industrial design.

Compare this to a typical university degree today, where much time is spent understanding theory in a specific field. Instead of a T-shaped education, you end up with a V-shaped education.

Rather than building a broad base, it lightly touches modules in other disciplines to satisfy the "multidisciplinary approach" advertised. We may take one or two modules in other academic disciplines, pass the tests required, and then fail to apply the lessons learnt. It fails to give you a broad, true, foundation, upon which you build greater depth in your chosen field.

So, what would the T-shaped Gen Z look like? Like Fig. 1.2.

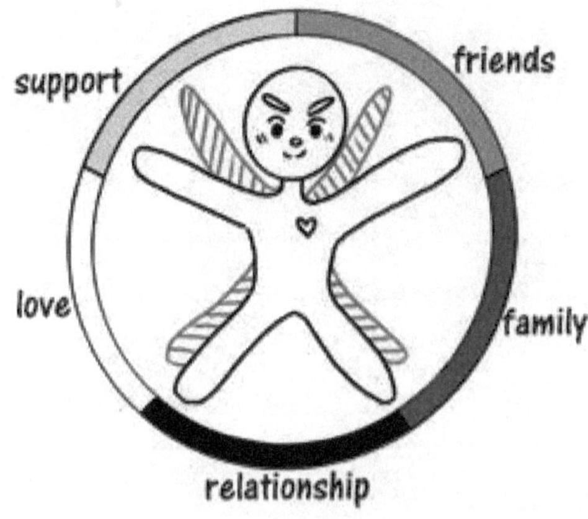

Fig. 1.2 The T-Shaped Gen Z.

At the heart of the T, is your character. Your character is the first thing to be clear on. This is your personality and your values. It's knowing who you are as a person before you go out to say that you're someone who can add to a job.

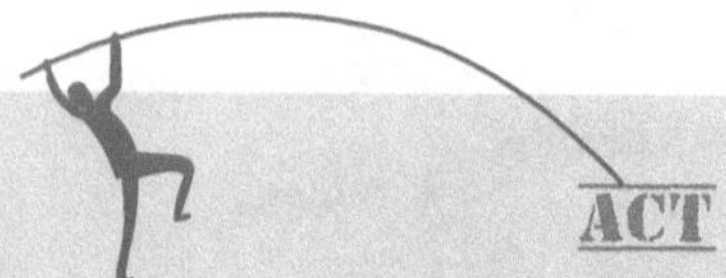

Take the PrinciplesYou test from Ray Dalio.
This will give you "detailed assessments of thinking style, including tendencies, talents and opportunities for growth". It will also explore your core traits and how you will use them in real-life situations. In this manner, you will be able to "see your tendencies in action and get the right guidance to help you achieve your goals". Find out more at:
https://principlesyou.com/

The hands of the T-shaped Gen Z represent your strengths and what you create with your hands.

Succeeding is broadening your *knowledge* and understanding for different domains, *and* deepening your skill in a particular area.

Honing your skill in one or two areas like a craftsman, and becoming exponentially better than the rest, becomes your significant value-add.

On the other hand, having a broad base of knowledge from different areas builds a cross-lattice of knowledge that adds a unique-layered lens of looking at the world. Billionaire investor Charlie Munger has repeatedly credited his financial success to his ability to combine knowledge from physics, biology, and architecture, which you may have thought of as irrelevant to something such as finance.

Lastly, it's the building of supportive relationships around you to become the springboard for your wider work. This is why there is a circle around the T, to remind you that there's always someone surrounding you, no matter how down you feel.

Taking such a construct to understand yourself is contrarian. Firstly, rather than keeping things on a conceptual level, a better schooling in adulting starts with prototyping projects you're interested in. Apply what you learn. Use your hands to bring life to what you have in your mind.

This goes against the grain of what we learn growing up, where the conventional wisdom is to plan what we want to do. There's no set path in adulthood. It's about trying until you find what works. Being willing to constantly prototype different interests helps you better adapt to adulthood.

Secondly, it's being clear on your core, so you can courageously adapt to different domains and industries. Rather than rigidly sticking to the domain of knowledge you were trained for, you go further outwards to extend yourself into areas you're unfamiliar with. Your depth of expertise in your skill allows you to combine this with a breadth of knowledge in different areas, making you more flexible.

We have now established the basic construct of the T-shaped Gen Z through which you can see yourself fitting into the work you do.

But ultimately, this will require you to pursue your own dream, rather than someone else's.

NEVER SETTLE

Never settle for anything less than your dreams. Please. The graveyard of dreams is a wide expanse filled by people who have chosen to give up their dreams to 'be realistic'.

Come along now. I want to show you something.

It's my room. There're shelves lining the wall, filled with all kinds of self-development books. There's a small table facing the wall. It's the table I sit at to write. There're ink splotches over the table, and notebooks strewn messily across different corners of my room.

My bed is in a corner. Under my bed are 22 stacks of cards. Those were the very first set of writings I published, under a postcard series named "One Day At A Time". It was no Penguin Publishing. It was published in a publishing house … in my house.

Don't laugh.

Guess how many I sold.

Five. The rest?

I had to give them away. I spent $2,500 on that project, printing 500 copies, only to have them barely see the light of day as they hid under my bed. After that project was published in October 2020, I nearly gave up. How could a writer sell only five copies? Was I that bad?

They say a leopard never changes its spots. So in September 2021, I published another book. This time it was worse.

Guess how many I sold this time.

Two.

I had spent $5,850 to work with a designer, and this time I sold two. Two! Surely my writing couldn't be that bad?!

In October 2021, I left my full-time job. With no job lined up, I had no idea what I would do. All I knew was that I didn't want this particular job. I had enough of meeting people's expectations of me, and never meeting my own expectations of myself.

As I explained to friends about how I was writing to make a living, I remember one shooting back, "Yes, but how long can you live on that?"

This time, it seemed only realistic to give it up. After all, with only seven copies of my books sold, it was time to face the reality of feeding myself.

But I persisted. It was like a dog never letting go of its bone in its mouth, constantly shaking and pulling to free it from the joint the bone was attached to. Four months later, in February 2022, I finally earned more than I ever did in my full-time job.

Sure, I had no idea how long this would last. Sure, it didn't sound realistic to be depending on gigs, where clients might disappear if they didn't like you.

But I've never been happier in my life. For the first time, I feel fulfilled and excited about what I do. It's not "just a job"; it's become a way of life.

I'm not saying that you shouldn't care about being realistic. But being realistic is not very life-giving.

When you first start bringing your dreams to life, it will be difficult. As tiger mother Amy Chua once shared with Angela Duckworth, the researcher who studied grit and wrote a book on it: "Just because you love something doesn't mean you'll be great. Not if you don't work. Most people stink at the things they love."

Hear that? You will *stink* at the things you love. Living your own dream means being willing to go through the stink of suffering to make those skills better. It is painful. But when it hurts, are you going to run away from developing your skills?

Don't live a life whereby you regret, and think, "What if …". It's the worst kind of life to live. This is the time of your life where you have few commitments, and you can try. You have no babies that require feeding.

There's no better time than now.

This chapter has explored the principles for adulting effectively, understanding yourself before you understand what kind of work fits you. In the next chapter, we look at the kind of work that will attract you and help you to grow.

2

ATTRACTION

When you first look for jobs, you may be attracted by the headline figures, such as the pay, the perks, or the possibility of quick promotions. But beyond the external attraction of a job is also how it fulfils you internally.

Thus, attraction, from the employee's perspective, comprises of internal and external elements. But with so many things to consider, sometimes we land up in the Cross-Matrix of Confusion, where there are seemingly thousands(!) of nuances to think through.

How do you know what you're attracted to? What should you even be considering as factors?

This is where a compass can help.

Beyond the initial attraction, *sustaining* the attraction is also vital. It's like a fire. Whilst the initial spark can raise a fire, the fire needs to be kept going with constant infusions of wood. Similarly, sustaining your attraction to a particular type of work is about constantly finding things that reignite the fire within.

To understand what engages a person internally, we had a chat with Shaiful.

FIND WORK THAT FEEDS YOUR SOUL: SHAIFUL'S STRUGGLE

Shaiful's story reads like something out of a drama. From being in six-figure debt, today he's the programming manager at Crane, a co-working space. It seems like a complete transformation.

Today, we are in one of the counselling rooms. Nestled in a comfortable sofa with nicely-scented candles in a corner, Shaiful leans back. He's dressed in a loose shirt, with a different sense of style. His pants are fashionably tucked into his socks. This is his off day, but he's still back to clear some work.

We kick off the interview with a question about his career history.

"I hate the word 'career'. For me, I prefer the word 'occupation'. Occupation is what you do. The word 'career' is dangerously insulating.

"I had to leave school after O levels because back then, when I wanted to study art, it was too expensive. So, I started as a cleaner.

"Later, I created my own zine. After that, I was actively gigging as a theatre performer for schools. Eventually I landed up in a theme park, 'pretending' to be a palaeontologist. That was fun.

"But I became a victim of my own success. I was earning a good pay. So I opened credit cards. I landed up with a 6-figure debt. That was a dark time of my life. I landed up having to do a DCP (Debt Consolidation Plan). Then somehow or other, I landed up here."

But how has he found fulfilling work?

"I'd like to start with the simplest question. Ask yourself, 'If you could do something in your life, what would you like to do?'

"So many of us side hustle to satisfy our soul. So many of us feed our stomachs, but we don't feed our souls. We need to feed our souls."

Have you fed your soul?

Your response to that question may fit one of two different groups. Either you've found great work that you love, or you're on your way to finding one that you love. The process of finding one, or even being attracted to one is not easy.

That's where this chapter comes in. Being attracted to work is no easy process. After all, if you had money you could live on, why work?

As the School of Life observe in their book, *A Job to Love*, for most of history, we did work that we would rather not do. Sowing seeds. Or emptying chamber pots. You get the idea. A good life was seen as one that didn't involve work.

But somehow, as we came into modernity, the idea that one could enjoy one's work, and make a living out of it, came into being. What was once seen as two complete ends of the spectrum—with one end being making money and the other "feeding one's soul"—became parts of the same whole.

How does one find work that one is attracted to, naturally? Rather than feeling like work is something that one has to constantly drag oneself to?

Let's start with some myths many have about finding work one is attracted to from within.

YOU FIND YOUR LOVE

One of the biggest misconceptions towards working at something you're attracted to is the idea that you will "find your passion". Proponents of such an approach suggest that if you reflect on certain questions, take career tests, you will find out what you like, and who you are like. They then suggest jobs you should explore.

Such a "passion" approach can work, but does not produce as much insights as a *"project"* approach. There are two reasons why. The first is because "finding your love" relies a lot on your feelings. It depends on exercises such as reflections on how you've felt about previous work you did. Those feelings can and will change.

There's little objective evidence that your feelings will be a reliable guide towards finding work that you remain attracted to, and especially when that work is layered with possibly nasty colleagues, a poor salary, or a long commute. In Cal Newport's book, *So Good They Can't Ignore You*, he questioned this "passion hypothesis". Speaking to an employee who followed his passion to become a monk, Newport found that this ultimately led him to deeper unhappiness. Following our passion may lead us to think that there's always something better to do out there. That may be true.

But just because you can do *anything*, doesn't mean you should do everything.

The problem with such an approach, is that we may place too much hope searching for that lightning bolt of insight that we believe will bring us to sudden enlightenment about what we love. But waiting for that lightning bolt may frustrate you.

Secondly, what has happened in the past is no reliable indication of what you will be attracted to in the future.

A better approach is to use what Dr Brian Little suggests: using projects to elucidate what one enjoys and is skilled at. Look at what you're doing now. You may be:

- Learning to cook healthy meals;
- Building a new computer; or
- Investing your excess income.

These projects can reveal the skills you're using, and the work you're interested in.

After graduating from the A levels, I had little idea of what I wanted to do. I took the two years of compulsory National Service to plan large-scale events at an organisation I volunteered at. These taught me to lead a team, plan a programme, and work with stakeholders.

After these projects ended, I started "seriously" thinking about what I wanted to do. I read books daily, reflecting through questions that asked:

- What do you enjoy doing in your free time?
- When time flies by, what are you doing?

I read article after article, Googling queries such as how to find one's passion. But these articles failed to instruct me as much as those projects had done. I was close to tearing my hair out from the stress of finding the answer.

Don't make the mistake of *thinking* more than you act. Whilst it is helpful to think through such questions, it can be far more instructive to take on projects that you're naturally interested in.

Build a computer. Write a blog.

Whatever happens along that journey, document that process. Write down the difficulties you face, what you're learning about the process, and what you're finding out about yourself.

Something practical you can do when you're stuck with deciding whether to take on a certain role is to "regret-test" your decision.

Stephanié Say, a research scientist, admits that when she was looking for a job after her PhD, she fell in love with photography and thought of doing that as a career. But she immediately thought about the reality of the job market and how difficult it would be to make a living as a photographer.

She invites young people to think. "What are you passionate about? Because these days, we're so focused on our social network. You see people doing this, and think, maybe I should do that. But then we're no longer aligned to our centre. We're not spending enough time on ourselves."

In deciding whether to push ahead with it, Stephanié is similar to Deddy. She regret-tests her decision. She asks, "Do you want to feel regret or remorse?"

Regret is the feeling you get after *not* doing something. Remorse is the emotion you feel after *doing* something.

Today, if you're facing difficulties knowing what attracts your internal compass, take time to ask yourself whether you would regret the decision you take.

Finding your passion is less about the thinking, but more about the acting out of things you're interested in. Don't find your love. *Work* out your love.

PAY AND PERKS MATTER: STEPHANIÉ'S STORY

When you first graduate, you may be excited about the big pay cheque you'll get. After getting a few hundred dollars a month from your parents, you can finally get a few thousands from your full-time role!

But how important are the external-facing pay and perks you can get from a job in determining what's attractive to you?

Stephanié was once a PhD student living in France. She was looking for a full-time role in Switzerland as she wanted to live there after graduating. But with no networks in Switzerland, she had little way in.

To stay meaningfully occupied, she worked at McDonald's. If it's strange to hear a PhD student working at McDonald's, you aren't alone. I thought the same too! Wasn't McDonald's a step down from life as a PhD student? After all, having a "Dr" prefix in front of your name seemed to represent a certain kind of work and income.

Stephanié didn't see it that way. Despite the lower pay, she saw her part-time work at McDonald's as a means to be meaningfully occupied, rather than falling into a depressive spiral over the lack of a full-time job.

One principle that helped in her job-hunt is *humility*. At McDonald's, she had younger people as her superiors. She was responsible for cleaning dishes, tables, and the toilets. But it was also there that she learnt skills such as customer service and stress management.

Hearing Stephanié led me to see the crucial quality of humility. Despite having a PhD, she didn't think of any job as "beneath" her.

It bears noting. We may turn down offers with salaries that are lower than what we expect. But instead of trying to enter at a higher salary, getting your initial foot in the door will give you a chance to prove yourself.

That's humility. The ability to look past oneself and beyond the pay one expects. Not less of oneself, but more of *others*. And that is a crucial quality, especially in the first phase of work, where you are attracting employers to you.

No matter how good you think your CV is, the job market is very competitive. Jordan Peterson, in his book, *12 More Rules for Life*, suggests that a helpful gauge is to expect *1 interview for 50 applications*.

The constant array of rejections can cause you to go through periods of self-doubt. If you're not certain about what engages you internally and what the value you bring is, the job application process can be deeply distressing.

This chapter is about how to better understand yourself and what you're attracted to, whilst balancing that with the external attractions of a job.

Going into the job market without knowing what is important to you, and what you want, can be like wandering around with a blindfold across your eyes. You get lost. And you get nowhere.

But before searching for a full-time role, there's a caveat.

A DIFFERENT WAY TO THINK ABOUT EMPLOYMENT

For all the benefits of employment, there's a flip side.

In employment, you're trading your time for the employer's money. The employer dictates your agenda. You may not get to do what you think you're best at. As you're not the boss, you can't decide to abandon work you dislike.

As Jonathan Haidt formulated in his book, *The Happiness Hypothesis*, happiness involves five factors (see Fig. 2.1):

1. Your biological setpoint for happiness;
2. Mental hygiene to keep your mind clear, with behaviours such as therapy, exercise, and meditation;
3. The fit between yourself and others;
4. The fit between yourself and the work you do; and
5. The fit between yourself and something greater than yourself.

Fig. 2.1 A person's happiness is determined by five factors.

Drawing on the work of Mihaly Csikszentmihalyi, who pioneered the concept of flow, Haidt found that the happiest people were those who did work that drew on their strengths and yet were not too difficult for them. This keeps you in the ideal state between anxiety and boredom (Fig. 2.2 overleaf). You're at a place where the task is not too challenging for you to feel fearful and anxious about, whilst also being in a place where you're not bored by what you're doing.

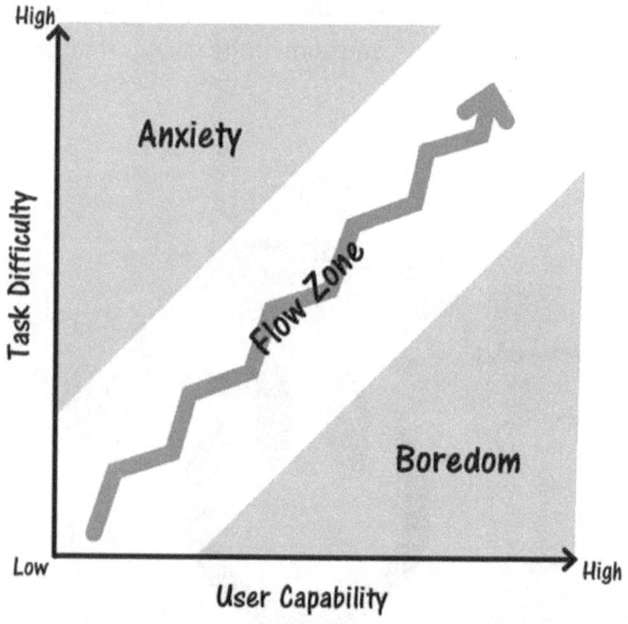

Fig. 2.2 The flow state comes when you're doing things that are just outside your comfort zone.

A helpful way to think of "flow" is to ask yourself whether you're meaningfully engaged with the task.

Imagine you were doing battle with a monster, with weapons by your side. Your skills are the weapons. The monster is the task.

Have you already given up, before doing battle, because you know that the weapons you have will never defeat the monster?

Have you mentally "checked out" because it's too difficult? In *The War of Art*, author Steven Pressfield writes about doing daily battle with the "resistance", who stands between him and the work.

This relates to your relationship with the work you do. Do you see the work as a worthy opponent, whom you're willing to do battle with? Or do you instead see it as too challenging a foe, that you don't wish to take on?

A simple question to ask is: *Am I doing this because I want to or because I need to?*

Wanting to do something springs from desire, a natural, internal attraction to the work. Needing to do something stems from an external obligation, such as knowing that you might be sacked if you don't do the work.

As a writer now, no matter how many missed swings I have at this "monster" called writing, I want to be in that battlefield, constantly sharpening my weapons for greater battle. Whereas in my previous work, I was fighting with a toothpick. I felt inadequate and incompetent. Knowing what makes you flow will make the difference between whether you're engaged in work or not.

Secondly, you're placing your security in the hands of the employer. It depends on how you see it. For some, that may be freedom. For others, that may be restrictive.

Growing up, I saw what could happen when you tied your security to an employer. It can leave you in a precarious place. Across the different financial crises, my parents were retrenched. We had to approach charities for help, getting free groceries such as rice, oil, and salt.

As harsh as this sounds, your employer may not care about your future wellbeing. They care about the organisation's well-being. You may end up giving your all, only to find yourself retrenched.

Therefore, before committing to a job, step back and think: *Might something different like entrepreneurship or freelancing work be better for me?*

Few people want to come to a place where they stand in line, asking for grocery items. Considering a life outside of traditional employment and building independence can untether your job security from that of your employer, allowing you greater independence. Whilst it's attractive to have the perks an employer offers, sometimes it's useful to step back and ask yourself if your freedom and independence to work on different projects is more attractive an option.

But if you still believe that employment is for you, there are three elements of an employer's offer you should consider.

THREE ELEMENTS OF AN ATTRACTIVE OFFER

I propose a different conception of work. *Work is what enables you to build physical, social, and mental wealth.*

Focusing on these elements brings us to look beyond the monetary compensations we get, towards a more holistic understanding of what we can get from work.

Let's first start with some common misconceptions.

More Work is More Wealth

Some may equate work to *wealth*. Work and wealth are different. However, in their minds: Work = Wealth.

The traditional narrative has been: If you work, you will eventually get wealthy.

Not necessarily. Work is a means whereby you exchange time, a finite resource, for money, an infinite resource. There are two crucial arguments here.

Firstly, money is not wealth. Naval Ravikant's definition of money is still the best I've found:

Money is social credits.

On the other hand, Ravikant says:

Wealth are assets that earn as you sleep.

In employment, you're exchanging your time for money which you can use in the future to get something you might want. You work for an hour now to get $20, so that you can buy dinner *later.*

Whatever you do now, is it building wealth, or simply more money? Think of yourself as creating a wealth, money-making machine that's able to churn out more and more money, *without* you tending to it.

Secondly, money is infinite. Because governments can always print more money. Time, however, is a finite resource that you cannot buy, sell, or find more of.

School teaches us to work harder and harder and that more work equals to more wealth. But it's not the case! That's why you see the CEO and the cleaner earning stratospherically different pays, even though they work the same hours. The equation "Work = Money" is not always valid.

Instead, when you think of work in this form (work ≠ money), you're no longer wedded to the traditional notion of work as one that comes with a contract. Society has taught us to seek a stable, secure income as the way to work. That's what work gives you in the form of a contract. A contract gives you the security of a regular income. It may not be the only way to provide for your means.

I hope this encourages you to break free of the societal narrative that getting a full-time job is the *only* way to be financially secure. When you look past that, you realise that the most important thing isn't for you to get a fancy job title at a famous company. It's to build long-term *wealth*.

Looking at work this way may encourage you to look at gigging as a possible way to work. Gigging is where you're your own boss, working for no specific company.

The traditional route of employment may not work for everyone. Today, you may struggle to get a job, because you're unconventional and unlike the other candidates out there. You're constantly rejected. If that's you today, you are not alone. Here's a fist-bump.

But you *have* something special. Focus on that. How special and unique you are and how able you are at generating value independently, rather than thinking of work in terms of generating value for a company.

Let's now look at the three elements that may broaden our horizons of what an attractive offer may be.

Emotional Capital

Emotional capital is building up an asset base in a Bank of Emotions. Building up this base of positive emotional assets at your job is vital. But then you might ask: *How would I know this when I haven't worked in that particular full-time job?*

It's true that you can never fully know if the company's culture will build you up until you enter a job full-time. But there are ways to sense the culture that works for you. Look back at your past internships, projects, or part-time jobs.

- What have been the types of people you've enjoyed working with?
- What were the qualities of the teams you felt energised by?

Grace, a lecturer on workplace relations at the Singapore University of Technology and Design (SUTD), acknowledges that it's hard to tell what a company's real culture is like unless you've been in it for a while. But she suggests ways to validate what you hear, see, and read.

For example, in the videos of the company's facilities, if the gyms or sleeping pods are new and shiny, it may show that no one is using them. Or sleeping pods may suggest how long you are expected to work!

Her next advice?

"Critically assess job descriptions. The more buzzwords there are, the more sceptical you should be. Whereas the more specific they are about a certain job role or responsibility, then the more "real" it's likely to be.

"Naturally, there are also websites like Glassdoor you can scan, or ask your own social networks. It pays to check first before accepting any job.

"It's not that the information is unavailable. I think it's partly because of laziness or maybe we don't want to know. Perhaps you want what's promised so badly that you're willing to close your eyes to what is there."

When you look at the job you're applying for, look at the job scope.

- Do the tasks involved make you feel good about yourself?
- Are those tasks that you have done before, and felt great about executing?

Don't take on tasks just because they are part of the job. Take on tasks that are part of *you*. The job doesn't become something you drag yourself to, but is something you wake up, excited to do.

Another easy way to find out about this is to look back at the times when you've done things for the sake of doing it, rather than because you were asked to. Look at your hobbies. How you spend your free time. You may find insights there.

Human Capital

Think of your personal human capital, as described below by Carl Richards, as three things:

1. Your time;
2. Your skills; and
3. Your energy.

These are the things you bring to a job. Think of it as an exchange. You're exchanging your human capital in time, skills, and energy for financial capital.

Realistically, you can only use your work to grow your skill capital. How? A job would ideally allow you to develop skills you want to develop, at an ever-growing acceleration. You would ideally want to be at a place where you find yourself constantly pushed to the edges of what you thought was possible.

In every superhero movie we watch, we love the heroes because the limits of their superhero power is tested. We see a villain that's big enough to challenge them. Would you watch Superman if all he had to defeat was a tiny ant?

We love Superman because we see him suffering at the hands of kryptonite, which saps his power, and leaves him at the hands of the villain.

In much the same way, in our own careers, we crave challenge. Not comfort. We want to grow the skill that allows us to rise to bigger and bigger occasions, fighting bigger battles, and entering caves where we have no assurance that we will ever emerge alive. That's what the best jobs do. They grow your base of skills so that you feel even more capable. To do that, ask for the opportunities that excite you. You don't get because you don't ask. You will be surprised at what happens when you start asking.

Whilst chasing a challenge can be ideal, balance this with realism.

Dr Candice Chee, the founder of MentorsHub, a mentoring initiative connecting industry leaders with students from disadvantaged backgrounds, frequently advises mentees to adjust their expectations of the first job.

"Many young people have the expectation that the first job should be their dream job. Young people have a lot of expectations for their first job. They expect the job to be high paying, to have a good title, good package, with a branded company.

It's important to be realistic in one's expectation. If you come with such expectations, your disappointment will always be there. The first job is hardly going to be your last job. The jobs that we get when we are young, are mostly stepping stones. Look at the first job as the opportunity where one can learn and get the exposure, to the industry or to the function, and learn from it.

"Build your experience, and your credentials from there. That will help you to move on to your next job. If you were to do this conscientiously, you'll be making very pragmatic steps towards achieving your dream job."

Dr Candice's advice seems contrarian. It's getting in to learn, rather than getting in to contribute. Doing the small things will grow your human capital so you eventually do the bigger things.

It's akin to the 20-mile march Jim Collins and Morten Hansen describe in *Great by Choice*. In 1911, Roald Amundsen and Robert Falcon Scott, two seasoned explorers, were competing to be the first person to reach the South Pole.

They used two different approaches. Amundsen focused on hitting a steady mileage per day, even though there were days when he could go more. On bad days, Amundsen still headed out.

But Scott chose a "lumpier" approach, pushing hard when the weather was good and choosing not to move when the weather was bad.

Eventually, Amundsen reached the South Pole first.

It's a story that holds lessons in finding what you're attracted to. Rather than looking for the job that offers you a big leap in pay, passion, or purpose, Dr Candice's advice is to view jobs as a steady progression to climb upwards or get across. The winners are those who persist at improving their skills in contributing.

Financial Capital: Ser Jing's Advice

One question Dr Candice often hears is: Should you chase pay or passion?

"I'd love to be paid for my passion. But, we all need pay to pursue our passion.

"Pay gets us started. But passion sees us through.

"It's okay to start a job that puts meals on the table and a roof over your head and work your way to pivot towards your interest.

"Passion can grow on you and the surest way to know if it will, is to be doing it. At different career and life stages, our needs change. One should be pragmatic while keeping your eyes on the horizon."

At this point, we question a topic that's often seen as taboo. *How far should pay factor into the attractiveness of a job?*

Money. What is enough for you? How much do you want to earn at a job to feel happy? How do you balance between passion and pay in choosing a job?

Pay builds up financial capital, which can eventually compound on its own. Money cannot grow if you don't work. But capital can.

How do people working at jobs also build up their capital? Could we come to a point where we were working because we wanted to, and not because we *needed* to? Now that's independence. You're unshackled to your job and can stop it when it no longer serves your needs.

To understand how others did that, I spoke to Ser Jing from *The Good Investors*, a blog written by two investors who managed to marry their passion for investing with their jobs as fund managers.

Ser Jing has a degree in engineering science. After graduating in 2012, he worked with *The Motley Fool Singapore*, which gives investment advice through online newsletters. He worked as a staff writer and also as a co-leader of the investment team.

I was curious why he chose this role when he could have gone into more highly paid roles such as investment management. After all, Ser Jing managed to grow his family's investment portfolio by an annual return of 19.5%, compared to 12.7% of the S&P 500 (Standard and Poor's 500). It would seem like he would achieve good returns (and a better pay) as an investment manager.

This is where Ser Jing steps back and shares his decision-making process in balancing pay and passion. After all, being thoroughly acquainted with the money people were making as asset managers, how did he stay away from that?

Firstly, Ser Jing shares a transformational moment in his life. In his early 20s, he had a friend from school who passed away suddenly. That had a big impact on his life.

"That got me thinking about the idea that nobody knows when their time is up. It's important to do something that makes me happy as much as possible.

"A lot of young people fail to see that your time here is finite. Oftentimes, I hear people say, "I want to try to make as much money as I can.' They end up doing something they have no interest in. That's a pity.

"If you don't know when your time is going to come up, you might work your entire life, however short that might be, stuck in something that you derive no joy from. Money may not always be everything in an attractive job offer.

"If we don't know when our time will be up, what is the best way to live our life? Or how not to live it? The best answer I have is doing things that I enjoy as much as I can.

"I craft my work in a way such that I minimise the unpleasant things attached to the investment management business. And make sure that the positives outweigh the negatives. So that in the process of monetising my passion on all the things I enjoy in life, I don't get burnt out. I put in the proper infrastructure to enable me to be in this for as long as possible or as long as my mind is functioning."

It's clear that Ser Jing doesn't want to be stuck doing something that gives him no joy. Whilst money is an important factor, he balances it with a pursuit of joy.

He told me, "Just a few days ago, I was telling my wife that I came upon this realisation that many work to earn money to do things they like."

It bears food for thought. Rather than trying to earn more money to buy things, or engage in experiences that bring you joy, why not find work that naturally brings you joy?

Secondly, to understand whether the jobs were truly attractive, he took time to understand different industries. He once knew a friend who wanted to enter the money management business.

"But when he entered, he became very disillusioned because it was not what he thought it would be. I think the mistake he made was that he did not try to find out as much as he could about the industry. He saw things from the outside and didn't understand what it's like from the inside. His career path could have been better if he had spent time understanding, finding resources online or physically, or meeting people. It's like understanding the actual underbelly of the Beast before stepping in."

But perhaps of greater note was how he managed eventually to build financial freedom despite working in a job that might have paid less than a mainstream, financial career.

To build greater freedom, he shares the story of his good friend's cousin. At one point, he purchased a very expensive vehicle. His entire income went into paying for the vehicle, leaving him with little to save.

It's a behaviour that he notices happens to people of all ages. "They make money to buy things to impress others."

It's a concept called the hedonic treadmill.

"People's desires often increase together with their earning power. But your material desires can remain stagnant over time, decline over time, or grow over time.

"The trick is to ensure that even if your material desires grow, it grows at a much slower pace compared to your income.

"Sometimes, your material desires overshoot your earning capability, even if your earning capability is very high. That causes people to be trapped. They can't leave jobs they dislike, because they are in debt. And they can't escape from that. Because their material desires increase so much, compared to the increase in their earning potential. That doesn't create the gap that enables them to be freer."

As you look at the job you're looking for, you may be tempted to pass on ones that don't pay as well.

I half-expected him to share with me ten hacks to getting one million dollars. After all, he is a fund manager. But his sole principle is to ensure that you spend consistently below your earnings. That way, you can invest yourself in a job you are interested in, even if it does not pay as well.

But the overarching idea is memento mori, remembering that that your moment on Earth is finite.

Finances are *infinite*. We can always have more of it. But time isn't. With that limited time, how do you want to find fit?

EARN YOUR OWN KEEP

Understanding what kind of job attracts and engages you is a long-term game. To ensure that you have the finances to last the distance, and not have to take a job that has little attraction to you, *build a skill that brings an independent income.*

There are two key suggestions in the above principle.

The first is "building skill". Naval Ravikant loves saying, "Become the best at what you do."

Keep redefining it until this is true.

Know what your skill is, and how to develop it. Many people live life trying to chase after the next "hottest" skill.

But it's your *natural* skill that will take you furthest.

Thriving in your transition from school to adulthood is a process of recognising what your skill is, developing that skill, and using that skill as a lever. Like a pole vault, you vault yourself over the swamp of adulthood.

That way, rather than wading through the muck of job applications, interviewing repeatedly, you are vaunted to a place that recognises your value, because of the skills you show.

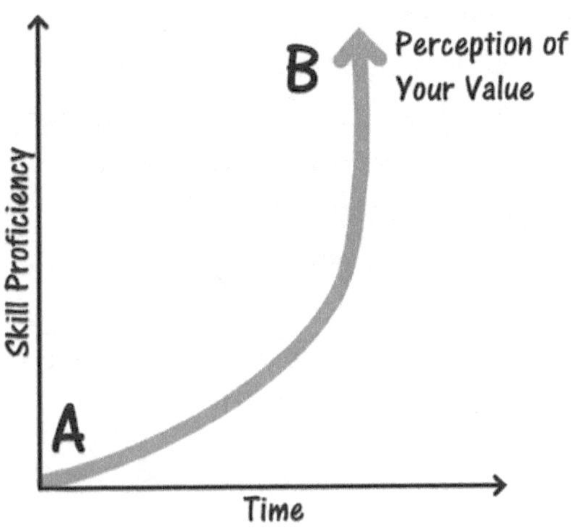

Fig. 2.3   The value perception exponential.

Value perception doesn't increase linearly. It increases exponentially. In Fig. 2.3, you can see more clearly what I mean. If you're starting out as a programmer (at A), your skill proficiency may be low.

But at point B, where your skill is much higher than average, you are valued much more highly. That's because you solve problems few people can. You create value faster than what others can. You deliver value far more reliably than others. It's why you observe phenomena like a Google programmer being paid $300,000 a year, whilst someone from Shopee might be paid $84,000 a year.

This sounds impossible. After all, as a young person, you may not feel that you've sufficiently put out a body of work that would make people go, "Wow, this is someone special."

But the internet has given you permission to publish anything you want, to showcase the value you can bring to the world. The only way to illustrate your value, and to vault across the swamp, is to consistently, and strategically, ship.

Shipping is about putting your skill out there for feedback. As a programmer, you ship a piece of code. Or as a marketer, you present an ad campaign that converts at rates above industry.

The missed opportunity in how we use the internet today is using it for consumption, rather than creation. We seldom think about harnessing the internet to hone our creative skill. Instead, we've used it to be mindless consumers of whatever the internet feeds us.

Gigging to Get By

Understanding the gig economy can teach us to earn our own keep. There are two forms of gig work. The first is freelancing, where you do something creative such as writing, art, or performance to serve a client's needs.

The other is through platform work, involving more menial labour, such as food delivery, driving, or last mile parcel deliveries. Many people choose this route because of the flexibility in work schedules and the quick payouts.

Besides, if you need to put food on the table, it's difficult to think about other things you can do to support yourself. No one knows how long it will take to find a job you're attracted to. It could be a week. Or a year. We never know. Going for something certain, like platform work, is attractive.

There's a caveat. You may be stuck there longer. Through platform work, you're doing something that may not grow your base of skills. After all, what can you place on your CV?

Please don't get me wrong. This isn't an insult to those who depend on this to sustain themselves. But you may find yourself further behind in finding a full-time role that leverages on your skills.

For example, Boon Lai, a university graduate turned delivery rider, told the Institute of Policy Studies: "You face a lot of hurdles as a rider in finding a job. Your resume is not really a resume because a resume should essentially show experience, but what is my experience the last few years? And being a food delivery rider, you don't have the achievement that will stand out from hundreds of thousands of applications."

There's also a murkier reason to understand. It's not in the best interests of platforms like Grab to ensure you get a full-time, professional role. If they do, they lose a stable base of platform workers whom they do not need to provide any assurances (such as retirement benefits) for. In a full-time role, where you're developed to grow your base of skills, this may not happen in the gig economy role.

In *21 Questions for the 21st Century*, Yuval Noah Harari argues that this produces an "underclass" of workers who follow instructions in an app, and no longer contribute creatively to the world. Platform workers have skills but cannot live out their full potential because they don't have the credentials employers recognise.

It becomes a vicious cycle because the longer they work in these jobs, the longer they stay there. It keeps platform workers stuck. Why? Because it pays just enough to feed you, whilst taking up the time, energy, and motivation you need to upskill.

Eventually, employers find it difficult to hire them because they cannot see how exactly platform workers can add value.

What then can you do?

Firstly, do the bare minimal to support your own needs. Calculate how much money you need to survive. Estimate the hours you need to work to reach that income. When you hit that number, stop working. Doing this allows you to devote more time towards developing yourself, finding a full-time role, rather than spending all your waking time and energy in platform work.

Secondly, know your skills. An earlier chapter shared how the first step to knowing yourself is knowing your strengths, leveraging that so others trust you with a job.

Thirdly, as Jay Ng from Weshine (mentioned in Chapter 1) suggests, engage in microlearning. There are online courses today that give you the chance to learn. Employers appreciate that. Take time to engage in learning employable, marketable skills.

Lastly, find a community. It will be difficult to find the motivation to break out of it alone. Going through it together with someone else will make the process easier.

Nurture Your Skill

To thrive in your transition, to truly fall in love with your work, nurture your work like you would nurture a relationship with another human being.

Treat it as a craft. Care for it like you would care for a gleaming jewel in your possession. Because your skill is your most valuable asset.

When you initially discover your skill, you will find that your skill level sucks. It's akin to playing the hard level on a computer game when you've trained with easy mode. You struggle. It's messy, you don't know what you are doing, and you wonder, "Are you sure this is my skill?"

Stick with it. Even if people say your initial work isn't great. As you develop your skill, the early work you produce with your skill isn't going to be great.

Keep practising. Nurturing your skill is playing the long game, not the short one. You never know when you break through, reaching a world-class standard.

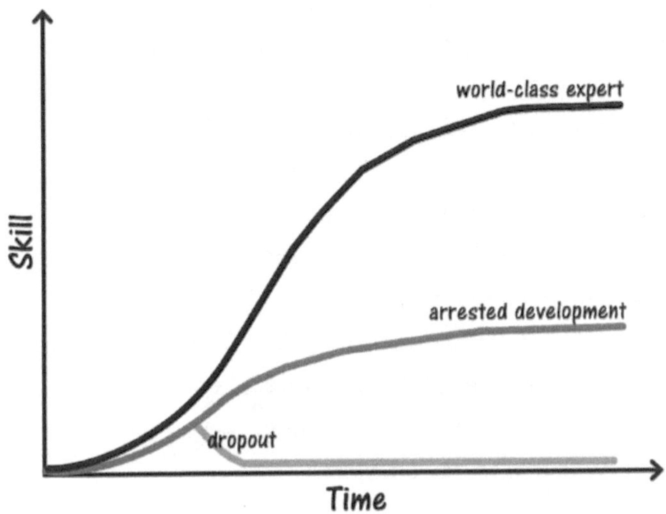

Fig. 2.4   A graphical explanation of how skill can grow over time (adapted from Angela Duckworth's book, *Grit*).

Starting out, there's a period of slow to almost no growth. That's the time when you're tempted to throw in the towel, and say, "It's not working. I give up."

But you will see yourself making certain improvements, or that over time, practice gets easier, and the products you're creating become of higher quality (see Fig. 2.4.).

Let's take the example of a complex skill today that many are learning.

Investing.

How do you get better at it? Practise, then perform. Rinse and repeat. Investing is one of the best examples of a soft and hard skill because of how it's an art *and* a science. Whilst having the technical knowledge to read financial statements is important, determining the quality of the company is more of an art. There is no exact number you can place on the value of the company.

Investing also has a clear measure of success. If your bet earns you more money, you've made a good bet. If it loses you money, there may be a problem in your process.

When you start investing, you may first learn investing from books. You may practise by making practice trades on a platform using fake money. Slowly, you make your first trade with real money. Eventually, the share price moves up or down. That's the performance.

As you practise more and more, you find your skill at identifying good companies, and investing in them, becoming much better. Your bets also begin to pay off more.

Fig. 2.5 Deliberately improving your skill level is switching between the learning/practice and performance zones.

Therefore, the important thing is to have a process whereby you practise and perform (Fig. 2.5), and reflect on that performance.

An Independent Income

The second suggestion in the principle of "building a skill that brings an independent income" is "an independent income".

Generating an income independently, without the help of your employer, is liberating. Even if you were retrenched tomorrow, you can still earn your own money. Diversifying your income source away from only your employer ensures you are not plunged into desperation when you're sacked.

Welcome to the world of freelancing. It's not as hard as you think. As professional speaker Yasmine Khater once said, "Clearly package your offer and ask for what you're worth."

Freelancing is recognising the problem you solve, and asking for what you're worth.

What are you offering? Do people want it?

To test if people want to buy the skill you're providing, start small.

START TINY

Bill Gates didn't start his career by creating Microsoft. He started with a small piece of code, typing out small programs on a machine.

He started tiny.

Tiny is transformational.

That's how you become great. By starting small. Super small.

As you look at where you are now, I hope the previous sections gave you a clearer idea of what you can be the best in the world at. Now, ask yourself if there are tiny behaviours you can do to improve your skill.

Try what BJ Fogg, the professor who inspired the likes of Instagram, suggests in *Tiny Habits* (see Fig. 2.6, overleaf). Place your aspirational goal in the centre. Let's say it's: Be a world-class programmer/marketer/investor. Then place all the behaviours that could contribute to that outcome. As soon as you write down those behaviours, write down what you think you can do to make that behaviour possible.

Fig. 2.6   According to BJ Fogg, a Swarm of Be(e)haviours will help you achieve your aspirational goals.

Next, ask:
- What is stopping me from doing this?
- What can make it easier for me to do this?

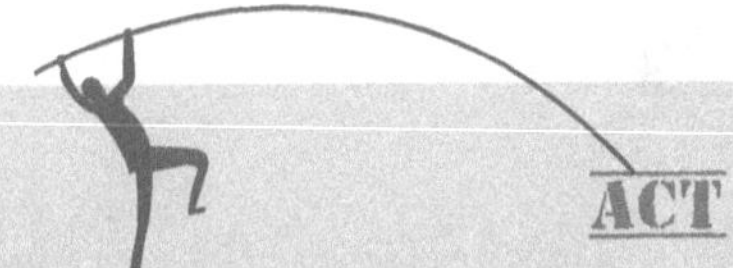

Commit to doing the small action that will contribute to the outcome you want. For example, if you want to be a better programmer, you could commit to writing 10 minutes of code daily. This small action seems so tiny that it almost seems too easy. That's the point. By making it easy, you make it done.

This chapter has spoken about how to understand the three aspects of a job offer—emotional, financial, and the human capital you will grow from it, to know if you would be attracted by it. But it's also provided practical steps on how you can thrive in the meantime, whilst you find a role that attracts you.

3

RECRUITMENT

The past two chapters focused on the work you need to do internally to understand what attracts you and who you are.

This chapter looks at the four stages in recruitment.

- Application through cover letter and CV;
- Interview;
- Post-interview; and
- Offer.

Many books already teach you how to do each stage. I'm not here to go over tried and tested ground. Instead, I want to encourage you to start from the back, from the offer, and work backwards. Here, I want to introduce to you a framework for thinking through the recruitment process.

This is the Slide-Step Framework (Fig. 3.1).

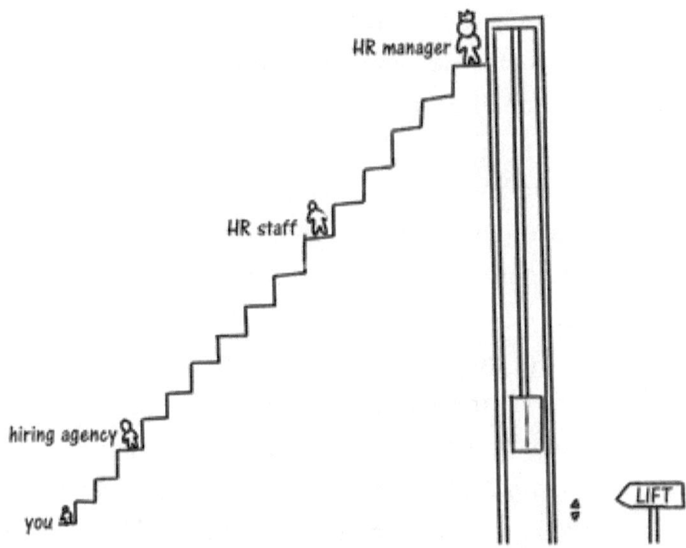

Fig. 3.1 The Slide-Step Framework encourages you to go in the reverse order, focusing on a relationship with the hiring manager first.

Often, we see recruitment as climbing a stepladder, from application to the eventual offer. But the Slide-Step encourages you to look at building a relationship with potential hiring managers, so you eventually can slide through the formalities of the CV, cover letter, and interview.

What you may not realise is that many jobs are referred to those within the hirer's existing network, rather than to a new, cold applicant that has no prior introduction.

Work *with* the slide, rather than toiling up the steps.

This chapter will share how others have gotten offers from selective companies in contrarian ways.

IT STARTS FROM THE RELATIONSHIP

People say, "It's not what you know; it's who you know."

To have a smoother job application process, it's easier to apply when you know the direct manager hiring. Develop a relationship with them.

Whenever employers hire someone, they are taking a risk. It's estimated that every hire costs the company a year's salary if they leave before six months. This includes costs like training and the managers' time.

That's why I'm going to suggest something radical to make hiring you more risk-free for the company.

Stop applying through job banks. Instead, spend time meeting people inside and outside your industry, who are in the positions that you want to be in. Ask if you can learn from their experiences. You will be surprised at how many people want to help.

This idea is from Stephanié Say (introduced to you in Chapter 1). It landed her a job when she first moved to Singapore. Not having any networks in Singapore, she reached out on LinkedIn to people in Singapore working in the industry she wanted to enter.

Rather than reaching out for the hiring manager, her advice is to go through "the small door". Sometimes, the bigger doors might be closed. Starting from the bottom, with people who are entry-level, might be easier.

Secondly, despite the ease of connecting with someone over Zoom or LinkedIn today, arrange a physical coffee with them. Shellye Archambeau recommends this in her book, *Unapologetically Ambitious*, which documents her meteoric (and unlikely) rise from being an African-American girl to the CEO of MetricStream, a tech company:

"Meeting someone face-to-face is an entirely different and a much more memorable experience. This isn't to say you can't build powerful connections online, but there's something about spending time with a person in all three dimensions at once that more solidly cements the relationship."

Meeting someone in person requires a greater investment of time from both parties. It also builds a personal and physical connection that cannot be replicated online.

This emphasis on relationships, was what eventually led Chen Jun to his role at Meta (previously Facebook).

175 Applications before Amazon: Chen Jun's Struggle

Chen Jun is fashionably dressed in a loose hoodie (immediately making me wonder if this is a Mark Zuckerberg thing), with a red Apple Watch on his wrist.

He passes me a paper bag beside him.

I'm surprised. I didn't expect this. I'm taking up his time, and he passes me a gift?

"It's the swag from Meta. It's cool. You can open it."

Well, I didn't expect this. I don't have anything for him.

Soon after, we begin the interview. Chen Jun and I met at an alumni event. When I first heard his story, I was amazed at how someone could have so dramatically changed his life around, within a year. This is his story.

"175 applications. I kid you not. January 2020 was the lowest point of my life. Can you imagine? I was this golden boy at university. I won scholarships, got into the top 5 in a national competition in China, and here I was, struggling to even get a job."

"That's why I always tell my mentees, 'Your university degree will not get you a job. Gone are the days of our parents' era when having a university degree guarantees a job.

"When I left my hotel management trainee job in November 2019, I had three job interviews on hand. I thought I would get at least one of them. That's why I resigned. But then Covid started getting more serious. My interviews froze. That's when I told myself, 'Get prepared to be jobless for the rest of the year.'

"Then in March 2020, I got shortlisted for the position in Amazon. I went for the interviews, and I got in!"

He goes on to share about how he followed up the role at Amazon with his current role in Meta a year later. He was actively connecting to people over LinkedIn messaging when someone he'd connected to recommended a vacancy at Facebook.

But what made him continue applying for the likes of Amazon, even after being rejected for 175 different jobs?

"What frustrates me about many people is that they say they can't get in, and … they haven't even clicked the 'Apply' button. I'm super thick-skinned. When I apply, I'm going to hunt down the HR's email address, the company's mailing address, and physically send them a copy of my resume so that they see it.

"Because they receive lots of CVs every day, there's no guarantee they will even see yours. I always tell my mentees to apply, no matter what they think of themselves. "

Chen Jun has very pragmatic advice for mentees.

"Firstly, use free resources. There are free courses online from Google that offer certificates, advice from Google about how you should write your CV. There are also webinars on the likes of General Assembly.

"Again, I'm not blaming the careers office, but the way they told me to write my CV just didn't work. They even told me to take a nicer picture! Your university may not help you get a job.

"Secondly, it's also networking. For me, there are two parts. Internal and external networking.

"At Amazon, even though I was at a low-level position as an account specialist, I knew people from all over the company. I knew people working in AWS, or Amazon Marketplace, and it was this that helped me learn about various aspects of the company. And to be eventually referred to their other contacts.

"External networking is using LinkedIn. I made it a point to connect with people in other Big Tech firms like Google and Facebook. I believe that when you're genuine and offer praise about a talk they did that you watched, people are more likely to reciprocate.

"It was this external networking that led me to this Facebook job. Someone I knew through LinkedIn told me about how Facebook was expanding their Global Ops team and suggested that I go for it.

"When I connect with people over LinkedIn, I'm always asking them about the culture at these companies and what are the skill sets I need.

"I have something I love to say to people: 'You need to be ready, rather than get ready."

But how has Chen Jun interviewed so well for him to get these roles?

"During the interview, there are no right or wrong answers. What interviewers are looking for are 'how you process' and 'what's your school of thought'. Of course, you need to know the company culture and values. But above all, you need to have clear thinking."

We are nearing the end of the interview now. I wonder if he has any parting advice for Gen Zs.

"It's never too early to start. In Year 1, you should already start thinking about the type of job you want and the skill sets you need to get that job. Again I say, don't depend on your university to get you what you want. Get it yourself.

"Secondly, quantify your impact. There was this format for CVs that Google taught: 'Increased X by doing Y over a period of Z'. You always need to quantify your value-add.

"One of the principles I took away from Amazon was to 'learn and be curious'. Start from being stupid. I'm not fearful of asking stupid questions. I'm fearless on approaching anyone. You can learn something from anyone. I take the time to teach someone what I've learnt. I believe that once you teach someone, you become a master at it.

"Lastly, surround yourself with people smarter than you. Being at Amazon and Facebook, I'm surrounded by people who are much, much smarter than me. At Amazon, I had a manager who told me to always think two jobs ahead of me.

"Another smart advice I've heard is how you don't have to be a CEO to be empowering. You can make an impact where you are. "

When we end, it's nearing 11:00 p.m. If there's something I take away, it's Chen Jun's consistency in connecting with others, not simply because he wants a better job, but because he's *curious* about what others do.

But it's also his mindset. It's the idea of never giving up on yourself, before others do. We do that so often, before others even write us off. If there's one thing I take away from this, it's Chen Jun's "shameless confidence". You never know until you press the apply button. Chen Jun chose not to give up on himself.

Chen Jun's emphasis on relationships leads us to see the wisdom of building relationships with industry titans. These "titans" can be your advisory board, caring and looking out for you.

BREAKTHROUGH IN DIFFICULT MARKETS: DR CANDICE'S ADVICE

Dr Candice Chee comes from a humble background, graduating "from the school of hard knocks". Barely scraping through the entry scores, and with little financial resources to enter university, she worked immediately after her A Levels.

Today, she runs MentorsHub, a mentoring initiative assigning industry leaders to mentees from less privileged backgrounds.

She helps students with low self-esteem and low morale to have a healthier concept of self, and eventually attain a career they enjoy. Along the path towards getting hired, people tend to focus on their lack rather than their qualities. This made them lose sight of their strengths, and rejections become a self-fulfilling prophesy.

One of the reasons why Candice started MentorsHub was to help young people in private universities have a level-playing field. She saw how hard it was for them to take night classes, whilst having a day job. Additionally, they faced mental hurdles, thinking that they were not as good as their peers from mainstream universities.

She tells me, "When I was teaching, I was quite bothered by the low self-esteem and low morale amongst some of the students I interacted with. Some told me that they felt like society rejects, having to fend for themselves. That makes me feel indignant … nobody should need to feel that way."

To help these youths, Candice and her team bring them through a self-discovery, reframing, and re-positioning process. Its Mentoring Retreat prepares mentees for mentorships, using CliftonStrengths to uncover the individual's top five talent themes and life design. The young people learn to turn their talent themes into strengths with subsequent coaching.

"We are born with natural abilities and qualities. We need to know that we do have self-worth which is not just defined by our academic qualifications. When we do not know our self-worth, abilities, or qualities, we tend to have a poverty mindset that [says] 'I don't have this, I don't have that … so what can I do?'

"It's important to know what these strengths are, so you can unleash it and make it work for you. One of the ways is helping them rediscover themselves. Many are surprised at the new insights they discovered about themselves!"

This enlightenment is the beginning of the emotional or mental breakthrough young people need to take the next step.

And the next step is mentoring, where mentees are paired with established professionals based on their needs. The mentors share their work and life experience, and help mentees embed their newfound strengths with pragmatic applications.

What are the practical things mentees must do to get a job? From her observations, Candice has seen how many may have been applying for jobs blindly.

"They think it's a numbers game, right? The more you apply, the higher the probability of you being called out.

"This is not a numbers game.

"I would suggest that young people first understand themselves, what they are good at, and what they are passionate about. Why do they want to apply for a certain job or assume a certain role?"

She recommends that young people improve the *quality* of the application, rather than the quantity of it.

"You're not just competing with your cohort but also with those who have years of working experience. It's very competitive. So, you want to ensure that every application sent out is of high quality and relevance.

"Enable the recruiter to 'know' you as a person, such as your qualities, motivation, what you're capable of and what you're passionate about, because a good job application will present you even before the recruiter meets you."

She believes every application should be intentional. It shouldn't be like throwing darts at a wall without aiming or practice.

Her other advice? Rather than focusing excessively on the outcome (getting an offer), focus on the *input*.

A thoroughly researched background of the company and facets of the job, aligned with how your natural abilities and life's experiences can contribute to company performance, delivered through a thoughtful cover letter, can make your application stand out. Focusing on input, rather than solely output, can help you engineer your chance of success.

Candice has this final advice.

"Success comes at a price. There are trade-offs. When you pursue those dreams, ask yourself what does it cost you? What must you give up or sacrifice? Time? Health? Relationships? Integrity? You must know your threshold, the boundary you will not cross."

Hearing from Candice, there are three myths of the job application process she points out.

Recruitment is a Numbers Game

People like to say recruitment is a numbers game. The more you apply, the more opportunities you get. It's not.

As Candice shared, it's the *quality*, not the quantity of applications that matter. If the CV was the company's first interaction with you, how would they think of you if you were sending your emails en masse to every company with a vacancy?

I laughed when Candice shared this, because I remember the time when I sent the same cover letter to two organisations, without changing who it was addressed to.

As expected, I wasn't invited for an interview.

There is no changing a first impression.

I can testify to this. After 91 applications and 20 failed interviews. It's not a numbers game. I'm not closer to the job I want. In fact, I'm further away. Over the past few months that I've applied for jobs, I've done so in a non-targeted way. I've applied across different job functions: project management, corporate communications, research, marketing, fundraising, training, business development.

My training was in social work. After two years in direct social work practice, I realised this wasn't my strength.

But applying in this scattered manner pulled me in different directions, rather than putting me in a place where I was steadily putting one foot after another, moving closer towards my goal.

Deep inside me, I feared going all-out for what I wanted in organisational development (OD). Rather than focusing on getting into an OD role which excited me, I was guilty of self-sabotage. I would apply for roles I wasn't very interested in, agree to interviews, but fail to prepare. I would be rejected. It was wasting the time of both parties.

Why do this? It was easier to pretend that I didn't want something, than to feel the full weight of disappointment crushing me when I failed. I could give myself the excuse that I didn't wholeheartedly want the role in OD, because I was applying for other jobs anyway.

But why would I prepare less thoroughly if I wanted the role so much? Deep within, I was ashamed of my dreams. Multiple people had told me to be realistic, and that holding such a dream was "dumb". Rather than focusing on the small universe of jobs in the role that I wanted, I self-sabotaged my applications to these jobs by applying for jobs I didn't want.

This might be you. You may apply for jobs you don't really want, because you're afraid that the jobs you *do* want would reject you.

It becomes a vicious cycle of self-sabotage, self-pity, and then self-flagellation. You sabotage your own chances of success by choosing jobs you don't want, and then make a half-hearted attempt to prepare for the interview. After you fail, you wallow in self-pity. You victimise yourself and blame the organisation for not hiring you. It ends with self-criticism. You punish yourself by saying self-critical things such as:

- No one wants me.
- I'm lousy.
- I'm never going to be hired.

The scattergun approach does not serve well. It moves you everywhere across the industries, rather than in a focused, stepwise manner. It serves well if you do not know what you're looking for.

The interview process can be where you find out more about what you want from a job, and what the general market is like.

But the scattergun approach may land you in a place where you feel like nothing is working out. It can be pure frustration. It's why you feel lost. Because you're not learning specifically more about any industry, but instead exploring every single industry. Like my math teacher used to say whenever we took a long-winded approach to solving a math problem, "Why do you put ants into your pants?"

You have my deepest empathy if this sounds like you.

Anytime you find yourself incongruent with your deepest desires, ask yourself why this is happening five times. This 5 Whys exercise is from Toyota, who pioneered this process to understand the reason behind the faults on the factory floor.

The first why may not necessarily yield the answers, but as you work through more and more whys, you find interesting revelations.

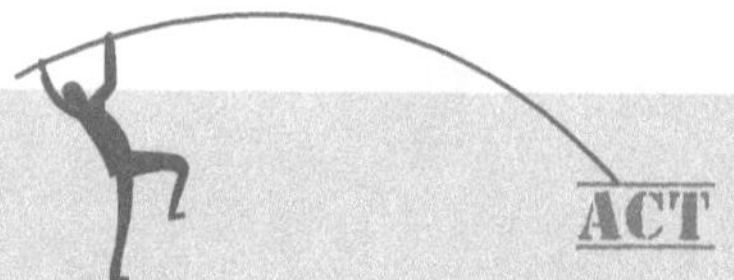

Do the 5 Whys exercise.
Here's a worked example.
Why am I so unhappy?
Because I'm not doing what I want. *Why?*
Because I'm scared that I will fail. *Why?*
Because I've failed in the past, and that was really painful. *Why?*
Because it led me down a path of depression. *Why?*
Because I tied my identity to my success.

The 5 Whys exercise may bring you in touch with your incongruence. After you better understand yourself, ask yourself if you should *stop* applying for jobs that are a poor fit for who you are.

Others say that beggars can't be choosers. When you're desperate for a job, you should not be choosy. I beg to differ. If you're desperate for a job, you should be even *more* choosy. It's only then that you stop wasting your precious energies on things that you do not like.

Secondly, focus on the 80/20 rule. The Pareto Principle states that 80% of the results come from 20% of your efforts. What is that 20%?

It's the focus on *conversations,* rather than connections. Reach out to people in roles where you want to be in and ask for a chat. That way, you get two different things. Firstly, you get to hear from them about what they did in their journey that worked. Secondly, you signal to them that you're available for hire.

In essence, forget the CV. Forget the cover letter. Focus on the conversation and build a relationship where potential employers feel they can trust you with work that needs doing.

You Need Paper Qualifications

The world is increasingly belonging to the makers. It's those who make something, and not only *talk* about making something. It's those that can ship, rather than simply have ideas. It's those that can *implement*, and not simply ideate.

The world belongs to the creators.

For those who talk about needing paper qualifications before getting hired, industries are beginning to recognise work products as evidence of the value you can bring to the company.

It's why companies like Google and Facebook use technical tests in interviews to determine the competencies of people, rather than solely relying on the resume. At software company Basecamp, co-founder Jason Fried does not look at the qualifications of potential hires. Instead, he looks at the work they have done.

It's in more traditional fields like academia, where the study is the work product, that may prize paper qualifications. Recognise that you don't always need to fit every qualification requirement to be hired for the role you covet. There are many times when we have this self-limiting belief that we are "not qualified", which stops us from applying.

Give yourself a chance before expecting others to give you a chance. Often, we discount ourselves before others have given our applications a look. Each application you do *not* put in is *definitely* an application that wouldn't go through.

But more importantly, create things which speak for your skills. Start a project. Write a blog. Make something that matters to you.

MYTH Any Company is Okay

You may want to throw your book at me (luckily I'm not in your vicinity!) when you hear this but: Maybe some companies don't match your ambition.

Not all companies are the right size for you. Before applying for any job, know what you want from the job. What is the scale of your ambition? Are you looking to be the top in your field, and therefore, you're looking for a company that has the scale of ambition to match that? Not all companies do. Some companies are okay with being number three or four, and doing enough business to survive.

Does the company you're seeking match the scale of your ambition? You don't want to be at a company that cannot match your ambition, nor put you in a place where you will be challenged.

I found that out the hard way. Growing up, school accorded 10% of our final grades to our oral participation in class. We were encouraged to question and contribute.

Coming to my first company, I questioned and suggested. One day, a colleague took me aside and said, "John, the problem is not that you treat this as more than a job. It's that others take it as just a job."

That's when it clicked. Others weren't necessarily here to improve things. They were here to do the job and go home. They were happy to get a pay cheque, work, and go home. A job was *just* a job. It didn't mean anything more to them. It finally dawned on me that not all companies are made equal.

That's why I encourage you to ask yourself what you want from a job and whether the company you're going for has the scale of ambition to match that. The recruitment journey isn't about saying yes to every offer that comes to you. It's also about saying no.

Don't waste your talents in a place where it won't be appreciated.

CLOSING THE SALE OF "YOU" TO EMPLOYERS

Traditionally, we see the dream job as a process where you:

1. Go to a job board;
2. Apply;
3. Interview; then
4. Wait for a reply.

This process may have worked in the past, but seldom works today. Today, the nature of getting a job is different. More and more hires are happening through platforms like LinkedIn, which used to be seen as a social media platform for professionals but has evolved to be the place recruiters go to find employees.

Furthermore, with the rise of remote working, you no longer need to be physically based in the same place! Fully remote jobs are now possible. What you used to think of as something impossible, like working for an MNC (multinational corporation) based somewhere you were not physically located in, is now possible.

Whilst it does refresh possibilities, it also increases the competition for jobs.

You're no longer just competing locally, but globally.

In the following sections, we will look at the practical things you can do to move more smoothly through the recruitment process.

How Do You Get Found?

Many people talk about LinkedIn. But rather than having "connections", have *conversations*. Chat with people. Keep talking to them until you get a job. Form relationships, not transactions where you exchange name cards, hoping they will be useful in future.

Secondly, apply with a cover letter. As Jason Fried and David Heinemeier Hansson write in *Rework*, a cover letter can't be mass-mailed. It needs to be personalised to each company. It also shows the company your clarity of thinking and communication. In a cover letter, to make yours stand out, include the following:

- Talk about why you want the job;
- Suggest a way they can improve.

How Do You Prepare for the Interview?

Every interview needs preparation. Don't wing it.

The first is using publicly available information on the company's website. Learn the names of the programmes they run, and what they do. It's even better if you suggest improvements to their programmes in the interview.

Secondly, as Chen Jun advised, talk to people working there to understand the culture and working styles. In your interview, name-dropping can work (if you've sought permission). It shows your connections in the company.

Thirdly, see an interview as a conversation, rather than a contest you need to win to get hired. When you walk into an interview, think of it as sourcing for a *friend*. If you enjoy speaking to your interviewer, it's likely you will love the time spent together working.

Lastly, prepare for the interview as you would a *performance*. You're performing to convince someone to entrust you with a job. Prepare the answers. Remember the right emphases to make in the interview. Record yourself. This may sound like overkill but thinking of it as a performance ensures that you accord it the necessary importance in your diary, preparing for it like how you would prepare for something like a marriage proposal.

A job *is* a marriage. You'll spend a significant amount of time in your job. It's up to 8 hours a day, 40 hours a week. Add in all the other times when you're worried about a work project, a colleague, or your boss. You will spend significant bandwidth on the work. Preparing seriously is the least you can do.

How Do You Close the Interview?

Following the interview, write a thank-you email to the interviewer. Beyond the basic courtesy of appreciating the time given to you by the interviewer, out of his busy schedule, it also reminds the person about who you are. In your thank-you email, include:

- Thank you;
- One insight you gained from the conversation; and
- The unique edge that you think will add most to the company.

Remember this. You're not just being hired.

You're *hiring* the company whom you want to work with. When you work for someone, you're taking on their baggage, their culture, and their future. You're devoting most of your waking hours to them.

It's like a marriage. You wouldn't go into a marriage without even understanding the person.

Do the same for any job that wants to recruit you. If there is an offer on the table, ask them questions, however sensitive they seem. For example, questions such as:

- Why did my predecessor leave?
- What is the progression within this role?
- What are the most challenging parts?

This can help *you* to also assess your fit with the company. As they say, "Interviews are like dating; employment is like marriage."

Before you decide to "marry" your employer, "built fit" is about offering to do work that's needed within the organisation, seeing if you can fit into the work they already do. It's also to see if you can fit into their team, their way of working, and their culture.

BEING RECRUITED TAKES TIME

Finding a job you love will take time. That's why being kind to yourself is vital in seeing this job searching process as a marathon, rather than a sprint. Listen to your heart and your gut, especially when you find yourself doubtful.

Ivy Tse, the CEO of Halogen Foundation, a social service agency that specialises in youth development, once rejected me for a role. She shared why: "It would have been easy for us to take you on, even though you may not have been a 100% role fit. But we are dealing with people's livelihoods here."

That struck me.

"We are dealing with people's livelihoods here."

There are many times, when out of desperation to get a job, you accept any job offer. That's not helpful.

No job is better than a *bad job*.

Think of it this way. You'll spend a minimum of three months understanding what the role does, what is required of you, and how to do it well. If it's not a natural fit from the start, taking it because you need the money is a recipe for disaster.

Hold out for a great fit, rather than one that makes you go "meh".

If you find yourself unexcited by the prospect of working for the company, right from the outset, you may find yourself better off rejecting the offer that comes to you and holding out for one that is truly exciting.

But how do you hold on, if the jobs you apply for continually reject you?

Holding onto hope

After rejection number 64, I went for a walk to unwind. I ended up crying. I wondered what it was about me that made it so difficult for others to employ.

There will be days like these during your job hunt, where you wonder what it is about you that employers are rejecting. It's easy to grow resentful, and to nurse a sense of resignation. Before we look at how to address these emotions, looking at what these emotions are can help you better understand what you're facing.

There's rejection. Then resentment. Lastly, resignation.

Rejection is the feeling that something you're offering is not accepted. It's psychologically painful because you took the risk of offering your skills to the company, but employers don't seem to prize it as highly as you do.

To illustrate this in clearer terms, let's take the context of a romantic relationship. Well, I would know because I've been rejected countless times. (If you have someone to introduce, please feel free to contact me … I'm joking.) You offer something as precious as your love. But it goes without being *received*, and without getting the response you want.

In a job, you offer your blood, sweat, and tears to give your all for an employer. But somehow, they turn it down. They say, "I'm sorry you weren't selected. All the best in your future endeavours."

Sometimes, the worst thing isn't the rejection. Often, you don't even know that you're rejected. You're left in limbo as you wait for the news. You keep waiting. That's often the most unhelpful part of the job application process, where they say they will get back to you, but never do.

You've taken effort to prepare yourself, to go for the interview, and yet they are still rejecting you? What is wrong with *me*? That's often the first question we ask. We ask what's wrong with us, rather than reframing it as: "Maybe it wasn't about you. Maybe it is about the company."

Next time you're tempted to ask what's wrong with you, following a rejection, reframe it as "maybe there's nothing wrong with me. It just didn't work out."

The other two emotions that feature are resentment and resignation. Resentment is feeling anger towards someone else. You feel a sense of injustice, that it's not fair. In a job hunt, you may find yourself saying, "It's not fair that they didn't choose me! I fitted everything they wanted on paper!

Resignation is wanting to "give up". You've given up hope that better is possible. You've thrown in the towel.

If that's you today, wherever you are, here's a hug.

You've done well. Incredibly well. You're incredibly brave for not giving up, for persisting, for gritting your teeth and pushing through.

Yes, I know that employers may be rejecting you. Yes, I know how they may seem cruel. They don't even bother to reply your emails, or pick up your calls. They don't even say that you were rejected from the role!

I want you to know that you have value, despite what everyone else says. You have value for simply being you. You matter. And you're incredibly precious. Just because people say no today, doesn't mean they will say no forever.

It's their loss, not yours. Don't lose hope of the value you can bring. I know that deep within you is a desire to contribute, to be of value to the world. That's why this hurts so much for you. Because you've worked so hard, and yet no one seems to recognise the value you can bring.

The question is: What are the practical ways to hold onto hope when it's easier to let go of it?

Here are two.

Firstly, you may be tempted to ask, "What's wrong with me?"

Reframe it as "What's not working at the moment?" There are lessons from each rejection. Reframing it as "not working" rather than you being "horrid" builds lessons, rather than dead ends. It's a reminder that each "no" takes you closer to the "yes", because you're learning from it.

Secondly, each day, remind yourself of the value that lies in you. With rejection after rejection, you may take it personally, wondering what it is about *you* that people find so difficult to employ. But it may not be about you.

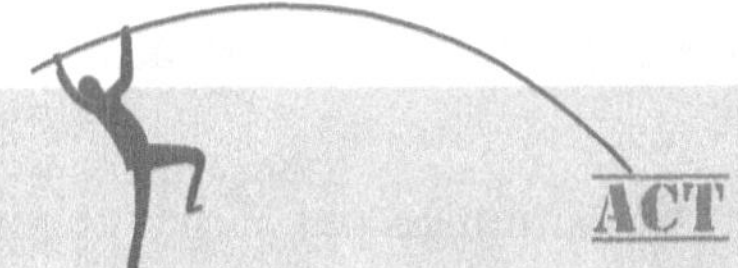

Write a letter of love to yourself to celebrate the qualities you see in yourself, and how you've shown up these qualities in the past.

Thirdly, Dr Candice believes in not wallowing in self-pity. That's what we may do upon rejection. We blame the situation or the people around us for what happened. We victimise ourselves, seeing ourselves as helpless within the circumstances that we are in.

She says, "You can feel upset. That's normal. But snap out of it quickly, and get on with life. It's important to be self-motivated and self-driven. Because when you are in the doldrums, there may be nobody who can help you but yourself.

"You may not have the resources, or the connections.

"When I didn't have money, I borrowed and read a lot of books, because that helped me acquire knowledge, broaden my perspective, and learn different skills.

"Secondly, be resilient. Each time you meet with failure, just pick yourself up and go again. Take failure as a learning point.

"Next, persevere. If you believe in something strongly, you need to persevere. There's a difference between perseverance and resilience. 'Perseverance is the persistence in doing something despite the difficulty or delay in achieving success' whereas 'resilience is the capacity to recover quickly from setbacks and spring back into shape'.

"Lastly, be comfortable in your own skin. Don't try to be somebody you are not. If you keep trying to be somebody else, you will never be happy, because it's just not you."

But there are times when you cannot get out of the rut yourself and need help.

WHEN TO GET PROFESSIONAL HELP

This book was written because I wished something like it existed at my lowest point.

As a 21-year-old, I was lost. I lost my dreams of being a doctor after my A Level results were less than ideal.

For two years, I volunteered my weekends towards organising committees to make my CV look better. I hoped medical school would take me in via discretionary admissions after seeing my (brilliant!) community contributions.

But they didn't.

That's when my world fell apart. I actively considered suicide. After all, what was the point of living when I couldn't live out my dreams?

That evening, after sharing my thoughts with a counsellor over the phone, he suggested going to the GP (general practitioner). The GP sent me to the Institute of Mental Health (IMH) to ensure I was safe, and that I was not about to harm myself.

That was the night things got worse. I thought this was it. My "clean" record of not having any mental distress was now destroyed. I thought this would make it even harder for others to give me a chance.

For three months after that visit to IMH, I struggled. I was anxious. Worse still, I couldn't do anything about it. I stuffed myself with food. In a month, I grew by 8 kilogrammes.

The turning point came when I started teaching children in a tuition centre. Somehow, teaching reminded me that I could still contribute to the world.

Here was John, stuffing himself with food, *but* who could still teach!

Teaching reminded me that life wasn't over, and that I was still able to nurture the next generation with my work.

I'm fortunate I didn't die that time. But others have. Today, suicide is the leading cause of death amongst 20- to 29-year-olds. It's why this book was written, so you find practical handles of hope in what can be difficult times during your transition from school to adulthood.

That's why if you struggle with holding onto hope today, there are two suggested actions for you.

Firstly, do something. Anything. Find short-term work that pays the bills. Why? In the liminal period as you find your full-time job, having something to occupy your time and energy helps.

Having your entire focus on finding a job, and not having income, can be extremely distressing. But when you can provide for yourself, the immediate physical needs become a weight off your shoulders. Preserving your independence, and not having to go cap in hand, to your parents for money, can retain your sense of dignity.

Secondly, do something you're *great* at. Not just good, but *great*. It's what people tell you is something special you can do, that comes naturally to you. If you don't have a job now, find some way to get paid for the skill you're great at. This can be through freelancing, or even offering help.

For example, if you were good at music, you could offer to play in the band at a friend's wedding. You will be surprised at what you get when you ask. Doing this reminds you of the qualities you possess, boosting your self-esteem at a time when you're constantly rejected.

Thirdly, find therapy. As much as it seems expensive and unnecessary, see it as a mind manicure, designed to remove the junk that's built up in your mind over your life. It reminds you that even whilst others may reject you, you should never reject yourself. Before someone else values you, first value yourself.

FROM BACK TO FRONT

This chapter has looked at recruitment upside-down, studying how people secure offers, before moving to the first step of submitting CVs and cover letters. Rather than looking at the usual advice around writing better CVs, cover letters, and making better applications, job offers come down to how much employers trust you.

Building relationships with potential employers, and industry captains, will help.

Then at the interview process, as Dr Candice shares, it's having a mindset of strength, rather than deficit.

Lastly, you were given suggestions on how to hold onto hope when you're close to losing it.

In the next chapter, we look at the day you've been waiting for: Day 1, of your new job!

4

ONBOARDING

Your first 90 days will determine what your next 9 or 900 days will look like.

Often, there is no structured onboarding process for many employees. Many end up lost, floundering, and unhappy. That's why onboarding effectively is taking on the responsibility for onboarding yourself.

It can sound unfair. After all, when you were in university, there was an orientation programme. Or when you were in secondary school, there were teachers who could guide you along the journey.

But coming into your first day at work, you're excited to get going, and you realise … you don't have anything to do on your first day. Or your first week.

You're seated there, twiddling your thumbs.

Most people's first day probably looks like their boss sending them a list of documents, like boring work manuals, to read through. Or filling up forms to get your laptop. You're seated there, thinking, "Play me, play me coach! When are you going to play me?"

But you sit there, waiting, and waiting. As hard as this sounds, your first day may be day 1,000 for your boss. He's just not as excited as you are.

Taking your own initiative is what's going to end up being the more effective route to helping yourself get up to speed, fast. But before you start raring to go, hold on.

MOVE YOUR ATTITUDE

Onboarding isn't simply about doing everything that you're asked to do. Having seen many new, young hires, I often see them doing everything—from making coffee, to photocopying documents—in a bid to make themselves useful to the company. They don't stop to ask, "What does photocopying really teach me about my job?"

Essentially, onboarding is about learning in a focused way about yourself, your colleagues, and your company.

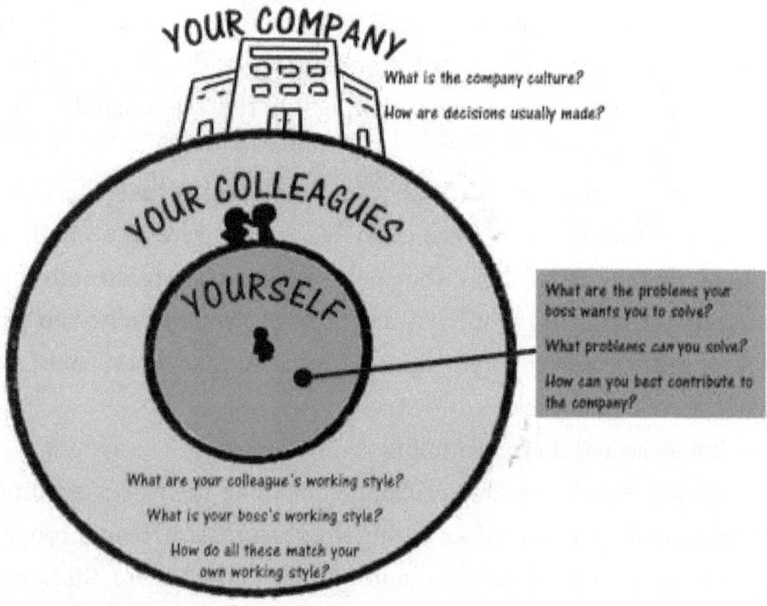

Fig. 4.1 The Onboarding Objectives Framework will help you understand what questions to reflect on as you enter a company.

This is where the Onboarding Objectives Framework (Fig. 4.1) helps. Understanding the three aspects of company, colleagues, and you, is accompanied by questions that can help you reflect on where you are in the process.

But for this to happen effectively, it takes three mindsets.

Openness

The attitude to approach onboarding is one of learning.

Stephen Krempl spent more than 25 years working in Fortune 500 companies such as Pepsi and Starbucks, in Learning and Development roles. He is an expert on how leaders can onboard their talent effectively.

In his book, *You're Hired, Now What Do You Do?*, he argues that being hired is not the goal. Making a success of your hiring is far more important.

But as young adults, we don't have a playbook for what to do once we get hired. We think getting hired is the goal. Once we get in, we go, "Uh-oh, what have I gotten myself into?"

Stephen often reminds young leaders he works with of this. "The number one reason the organisation hired you is to be a problem-solver. Your job is to solve a problem.

"Don't look at problems as problems. Many young kids go, 'Oh my God, there's so many problems here.'

"But that's the perfect opportunity!

"If your idea is that you have to come into a perfect situation where everything runs smoothly, then you have to think, 'Why did they hire me for?'"

Thus, the first thing to understand is what the problem you're hired to solve is. The difference between good and great employees, as Morten Hansen studied in his research of 5,000 employees, was that the best employees knew where their greatest drivers of value were. They focused on the actions that drove value-creation.

Think of a plant choked with weeds. Your job is to remove those weeds so the plant can flourish. The plant is the business you work in. The weeds are the problem. Your job is to enable flourishing. But for that to happen, problems have to be removed.

To learn better requires an attitude of openness. Stephen's neighbour, who was the head of supply chain management for a global company, once told him, "Here's my first line to the people I hire every year. I'll tell them everything you learnt in college, throw it out of the window. I'm going to teach you from now on what I need you to do."

Many of us come into work holding onto preconceptions from university. We think the theory we've learnt or the case study we used at university, offers useful advice for the boss. We may end up thinking that our ideas are great. We may tell the boss what you think he should do, rather than waiting for him to tell you what you can do.

As Stephen points out, it's the small things that count. It's the willingness to be small, to take an attitude of humility, and of being here to learn, to solve seemingly small problems well, that helps bosses eventually trust you with the big things.

Patience

Have patience. When Daryl Omerod, the CEO of the Students' Union at the University of Nottingham, started, he made no major decisions for the organisation in the first three months. He left daily operating decisions to the organisation's interim CEO. This seems contrarian, especially when you're at the top.

But with the Union being an organisation staffed by many young graduates in their first jobs, he encourages this patient approach for the young staff he onboards. He says, "The critical thing is to give yourself permission to take your time. Take time to understand the culture of the organisation."

Attentiveness

Understanding the culture starts with paying attention to what you see at work. There are three elements that Stephen Krempl, who conducts onboarding programmes for many of the Fortune 500 companies he has worked for, suggests that young staff pay attention to.

The first is how meetings are run. He says, "Most people think, 'I'm very interested.'

"No, you're not.

"If you're really interested, then you understand exactly what the problems your boss has. How are you adding value to them to try and resolve it? Or do you even give them access to things you found, in your research, to help them?

"Give them a reason to pay attention to you.

"How do you show that in the meeting? In most companies, the entire day is made up of meetings. What do you do in a meeting? How do you be interested and pay attention?"

Here, Stephen observes that there is a subtle, but important, difference between attending a meeting and being interested. Attending a meeting is sitting there and passively consuming the things that are said.

Being interested is actively learning and contributing to the meeting. You may not say anything.

But if through the meeting, you learn more about how your bosses think, interact, decide, and are influenced by others, you then learn how to better interact with your boss in future.

The second element of understanding the organisational culture is knowing what your leaders are like. "Do the research on the people you'll work for, such as your leaders. What do they like? Or not like? Senior leaders are not your age, right? How do they like to communicate? Is it email or text?

"One of the key things for most people in an organisation is how to communicate to people appropriately at different levels. Your colleague is different from your supervisor. And it's definitely different to how you communicate to your CEO.

"One leader may want you to bring ideas to the meeting whilst another may be going, 'You listen to my ideas, and you execute it.'"

"Every meeting you go to depends on who the person there is. Pay attention and figure out what their style is."

Stephen quickly adds that paying attention to their manager's style is not a task many new hires take time to do. But he recommends, "Just go and ask your colleagues when they're around. 'What does Mr Lim want? Or expect in his meetings?'

"How many people even ask that question? I don't think they do. But that would be the single best question they asked."

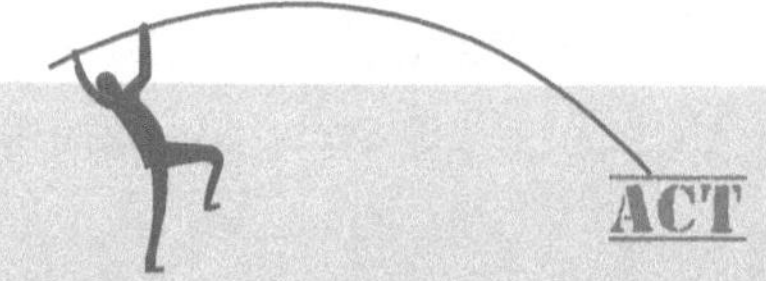

In your next conversation with a colleague, ask: What does our boss want or expect in his meetings? How does he usually work?

The second practical step is to have a buddy.

Daryl ensures that every new staff has a buddy. This buddy answers questions—like: How do you use the photocopier? How do you book this room?—but is also there to ensure that there's a friendly face.

The last step is to ask questions. As a professor once advised me, "The question is more important than the answer."

Questioning doesn't need to be out loud. In more hierarchical companies, your questioning might place you in a spot where you're seen as a young upstart, here to shake things up. It may put people off.

But you can question in your head. Build questions about issues you see and understand more about how to resolve them.

As leadership guru Michael D. Watkins shares in his model in Fig. 4.2, two things help in this period of questioning during your onboarding process:

- Focused learning; and
- Effective relationship building.

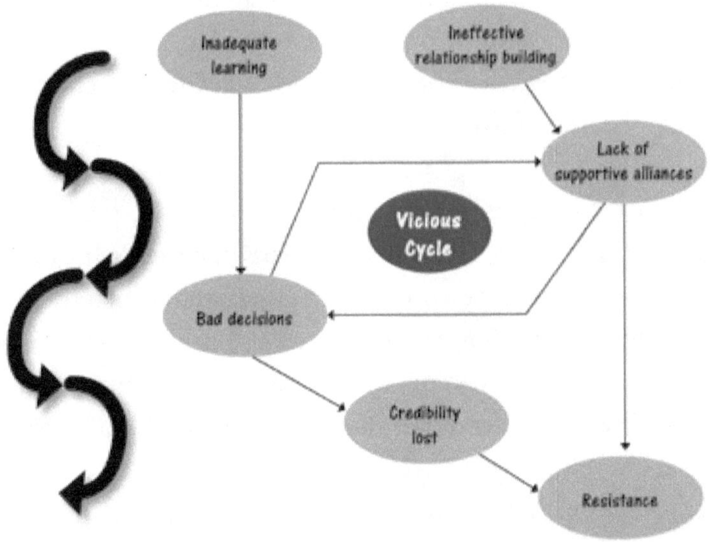

Fig. 4.2 The vicious cycle of transitions as highlighted by Michael D. Watkins.

That builds an effective foundation for you to start on your virtuous cycle of transitions. As we mentioned in the earlier Onboarding Objectives Framework, learn across company, colleagues, and yourself. In these three aspects, focus on the way things are done, decisions are made, and how people are.

Think about it as a science experiment! It's a three-step process of:

1. Having questions;
2. Building a hypothesis about why this is so (and where you can best help); and
3. Gathering evidence to support/refute your hypothesis.

The first way of gathering evidence is through observations. Use the quality of attentiveness! When you sit in on meetings and conversations, look out for small things:

- How does your colleague greet clients?
- Is there a set format for how meetings are run?
- How is work moved through the company?
- What is the process whereby work is handed to the person, and off to the next person?

The second way is through conversations. Take time to talk to people throughout the company, across the hierarchy. Take a position where you're there to learn and understand what things in the company are like. During these conversations, take time to build a relationship. What's helpful is to always qualify your questions by disarming your interviewee. Saying something like, "I may be wrong about this. But why...?"

Lastly, as marketing director Adeline Tiah suggests, "Have a 100-day plan, a moving 100-day plan. Many times, people focus on the first 100-days. But having a moving 100-day helps you be of constant value to your employer."

Onboarding is not an endpoint. Rather, it's a continual process where you're constantly adapting yourself to the next task that's being assigned, so that you're best prepared for it.

MAKE SOMETHING

All these initial conversations and lessons may seem like "pointless" work. After all, what is it going to feed into other than your own understanding of the company?

Building early credibility with your boss can start with explaining to him that these conversations will serve as an "observation exercise" where you eventually share with the team the key insights of how they work, and suggestions on working better.

An observation exercise was what Daryl embarked on when he came in. Despite the charity urgently needing remedies, Daryl held back. Whilst it was tempting to jump into firefighting mode, immediately suggesting fixes, Daryl took time to listen. He spoke to stakeholders, having more than a hundred conversations with different staff to understand the issues.

He shared these lessons in an observation exercise to his staff, and then later to the board of directors.

Curious about why he did this, I asked.

"These first 90 days would not come again. We need to understand what is, before we suggest what can be."

This played a big role in his eventual success in the first year, where he raised student satisfaction rates from 80% to 95% in one year.

MANAGE YOUR BOSS

To transit effectively to work, the most important relationship to build is the one with your boss. But there's a problem.

The Problem

Not over-management. But under-management. Management guru Bruce Tulgan observed how, over the last decade, more have advocated a hands-off approach towards employees, giving them "space to do their best work". Consequently, staff do not have the guidance to even know where the boundaries lie. Or what great work even looks like.

Taking charge of your relationship with your boss helps you get the support and structure you need. Don't wait for bosses to do something with you. It's about you initiating conversations with him, guiding him, asking him for what you need, and telling him what you don't need.

What's worse is that today, with many people remote working, it's harder to have that structured, developmental conversation about what's necessary with your boss. Everyone is too busy to talk to you, inundated with emails, messages, and notifications.

Why Should You Manage Your Boss?

Managing your boss sounds rude and disrespectful. After all, your boss should know better than you. Make no mistake about it.

For all the myths that we have about having a boss, the boss is a crucial factor behind you succeeding and failing in your job. But we have certain myths about submitting to a boss that puts us in our own way in succeeding at work.

High Performers Don't Need Guidance

During my first appraisal, I asked for a pay rise. Clearly, I thought I was a high performer. It was not until my boss told me to read the job description, and to follow the job description, that I realised that what I was doing was outside my job description. I wasn't even addressing my basic work.

It was like running before I tried to walk.

Before you think you're a high performer, get the basics right. Getting the basics right involves five elements.

Fig. 4.3 The Clockwork Model for exceeding expectations.

This is where the Clockwork Model (Fig. 4.3) helps you clarify expectations, so you can exceed them, consistently, like clockwork. What's also important is to note how this is a repeating cycle, requiring you to constantly circle round, to re-understand your boss' expectations.

1. Make sure your work fits with the company's overall mission;
2. Have goals spelt out and guidelines and parameters for your tasks made clear; and
3. Know the concrete deadlines, timelines, and reasonable performance benchmarks to meet.

We start first with mission. Before you come up with the next fancy idea, do you know what your company's mission is? Do you know what they want to achieve?

During my first job, I thought I was a high performer because I was introducing new ideas. Little did I realise that this did not square with the company's mission. The company's mission wasn't to reinvent the wheel, but to run things reliably. It wasn't looking to be a trendsetter.

My bold ideas didn't fit with the company's mission to provide services consistently and reliably.

This isn't about killing your ideas. But without knowing your company's mission, you may be banging your head against the wall. Even if you execute a new idea to perfection, in the eyes of your organisation, you may not be valued because it did not contribute to their overall mission.

One practical way to understand your company's mission is using Watkins' "5 Conversations". In his book, *The First 90 Days*, Watkins studied the key transitory challenges that leaders make in their first 90 days of a new role, and what they would need to do to succeed.

WARNING! Use common sense to see if your company is even ready for these conversations.

The first is the situational diagnosis conversation. This helps you understand what point the organisation is at, and what's needed from you. Table 4.1 is Michael D Watkin's STARS model to help you diagnose what stage your organisation is currently at.

Stage	Explanation
Start-up	Getting new initiative off the ground
Turnaround	Saving an initiative that's in trouble
Accelerated growth	Rapidly expanding business
Realignment	Re-energising a previously successful business that now has problems
Sustaining success	Maintaining vitality of successful organisation and bringing it to the next level

Table 4.1 Michael D. Watkins's STARS model.

The four questions Watkins suggests you can ask your boss are:

1. What are the elements of the STARS model you see in this current situation?
2. How did it reach this stage?
3. What factors (soft and hard) make this situation a challenge?
4. What resources can you draw on?

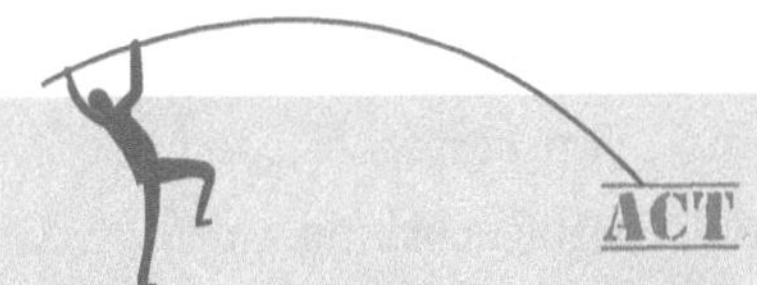

Start asking the Watkins' questions of a close colleague.

Understanding the mission and how you fit into that mission helps you move with greater alignment to your boss.

Secondly, know the goal. What are you trying to accomplish?

Thirdly, understand the guidelines to doing your work. How does your boss want the work done?

Some questions that are useful include:

- What are your expectations for me?
- What would be a great job in your eyes?
- What can I do?
- What can't I do? What are absolute no-nos?

Do you know what you can and cannot do? If you're not sure, ask. If you're not sure about where the limits of your autonomy and power lie, ask. It's better to be safe than sorry.

In a knowledge economy job, the degree of flex in your job and the variables that are involved are infinite. There's no way of listing out everything that's a no-no. That's why I say: Listen to your gut.

If you feel uneasy about something, step back and ask, rather than charging forward.

Someone once told me, "You have to remember that not everything is on your shoulders. Whose head gets chopped is ultimately not yours. It's your boss's, especially if something goes wrong. Making your boss look stupid loses you credibility quickly."

As much as bestselling author Tim Ferriss can suggest "Ask for forgiveness, not for permission", in the working world, asking to clarify whether you can do something ensures that your boss puts increasing trust in you, so that he can eventually forgive you when you make a mistake, rather than fire you.

Fourthly, know the deadlines to meet. This is not university. Deadlines come with real-world consequences. Profits may be lost, patients might die, clients might lose sleep over your late actions. Hitting deadlines, or renegotiating them when you cannot meet them, is imperative.

Lastly, your KPIs demonstrate what is a good job in the eyes of your boss. That is where an expectations conversation helps. That's the second conversation that Watkins suggests in his book.

- What does your boss need you to do in the short and medium term?
- What are the top 3 priorities for your boss, for you?
- How will your performance be measured, and when?
  You need to know:
- What to deliver (in what quality and quantity); and
- When to deliver.

An expectations conversation is a guardrail that steers you and your boss to know each other's expectations and align them.

It's not about lowering your expectations of your employer, but it's being clear that there are some which are reasonable, whilst others will never be met. Not communicating these expectations will set you up for unhappiness.

My Boss is Responsible for Telling Me What He Needs

Forget how you were treated in university. This is the workplace. And in the workplace, one useful adage is:

> No one is put on this Earth to take care of you.
> Except yourself.

This quote, from Robert Glover's *No More Mr Nice Guy*, is a reminder of how you need to take care of yourself. Remember how in university, everything was made clear to you? You were told what to read, how to write, how to structure your essay, and how to do it well.

You're not going to be told that at work. You need to ask.

Go back to the basics and clarify. Be humble. Say something like, "This is my first time doing this, and I would like to learn how to do this well so we can make work easier for us."

Remember, sometimes bosses have been doing it for so long that they forget that there was a time when they didn't know.

They might say, "Just try it. Have a go at it. Tell me how it goes." *Don't.*

Make a checklist for how you would approach the task, so that you can do it over and over again.

There are likely to be many different tasks you're going to be asked to do. For each task, ask yourself if you can break down each component task so that you can replicate the success of the task.

If you don't know, ask. Expecting your boss to read your mind, and to know what you don't know, is a recipe for failure.

As Bruce Tulgan mentions in *It's Okay To Manage Your Boss*, understand:

- Clear and reasonable expectations, with specific guidelines and a timetable;
- The skills, tools, and resources needed to meet those expectations or an acknowledgement that you're asked to meet these expectations without them;
- Accurate and honest feedback about your performance and how to adjust when things go wrong; and
- The recognition and rewards in exchange for the performance.

Yes, sometimes it is terrifying to think we are being let out into the real world with little idea how we're supposed to deal with work.

But if you don't take charge, no one will.

You take the first step to managing your boss.

REGULATE YOUR 1–1S

Managing your boss starts with being intentional about the 1–1s you have. Even if it's for 15 minutes, schedule it.

Many report that their bosses don't have time for them. In one story shared by Bruce Tulgan, a nurse couldn't get her boss. But she knew exactly when her boss would be at the vending machine so that she could get alone time to clarify matters.

Take time to do the 1-1, where you address:

- Your challenges;
- How you need help;
- Suggestions from your boss on how you move forward; and
- Upcoming work projects you're worried about.

Despite being more connected than ever, we seem even more disconnected from our bosses than ever before. Management is no longer the high-touch method to manage employee's performance, but has become seen as something "bad", because workers are assumed to need more flexibility and autonomy in the 21st century.

Nope. Tulgan's survey of 4,000 Gen Zs found that supportive leaderships were still the most highly ranked job factor (Fig. 4.4, overleaf).

Fig. 4.4 Job factors ranked in order of importance, according to the results of a survey done by Bruce Tulgan.

To onboard yourself more effectively, ask for what you need, in a structured and intentional way. Expecting your boss to do that for you may have worked if you were in primary school … but that's not where you are. You're an adult now. Personal responsibility for what you need is key.

5

RETENTION

Now that you're past your first three months, the next three months (or years), may present different challenges. That's when you begin to deal with issues such as your first probation, and then … boredom. Passing your probation is often the mark when people get increasingly bored. There doesn't seem to be anything else to work towards after passing probation. Eventually, you may decide to move on, seeking new challenges.

Millennials and Gen Zs are known for job-hopping, moving from job to job, always looking for something new. After all, things can get boring after a while.

This chapter aims to answer the question: How do you retain yourself in the same job?

For that, I spoke to people in jobs that seemed dull and repetitive. Like bus driving.

NOT "JUST A JOB": CE XUN'S ADVICE

When I first boarded Ce Xun's bus, I was surprised.

A soft toy of a cute cat sits near the window. Boarding the bus, Ce Xun greets or nods at you. It's a different experience to the many bus rides I've taken, where bus captains sport a dour look. Later when I ask him why he's placed a soft toy there, he tells me that it's to cheer himself up, and hopefully, the lives of others who board his bus.

I want to speak to him. Whenever we think of engaging work, we think of high-flying, white-collar jobs that fly us across continents, give us ping-pong tables to play on, and intellectually stimulate us. We don't think of blue-collar jobs like driving a bus.

How does he stay in a job that's seen as boring, dead-end, and perhaps blue-collar?

He didn't set out to become a bus driver. It was by chance.

He started out in a town council, handling municipal issues such as ensuring trash was taken away, lifts were repaired, and that people paid their fees. But after disagreeing several times with his boss, he left. Without a job.

That's when he decided to drive a bus, something he once thought of doing when he was young.

I ask him if driving a bus is his "passion". After all, it's the buzzword today. You would also think that passion would feature heavily in people who stay in their jobs. He admits that there are days when he's frustrated and bored.

How does he deal with the boredom of driving the same route, over and over again?

"I put aside the fact that it's the same route and tell myself that it's a job, I have to do it. I do it to the best of my ability, even if it means going beyond expectations.

"But I also see it in a different light. To me, it's a career where we move people from where they are to wherever they need to go.

"That alone, in itself, is important."

In *retaining* the motivation to work, Ce Xun doesn't even try finding the motivation. He admits that there are days when he loses his initial interest in driving a bus. He accepts that driving a bus *is* driving a bus. There aren't always going to be special days every day.

But he also reminds himself that the job can be more than a job, in how he can make every commuter's journey more pleasant. Like with a soft toy for the passengers.

"When you see something that's not normally there, the hope is that it would grab their attention and mentally distract them from whatever they're thinking. It's also a reminder to myself to take it easy, whatever situation may happen."

Clearly, Ce Xun has taken a different approach to what most people would take to a supposedly "boring" job. Beyond putting a soft toy on his bus, he takes time to acknowledge the people boarding his bus.

"We are all individuals. When people go about their daily lives, commuting home, they may feel 'I'm nobody'. A grain of sand in this big universe. So, I nod to them, acknowledge them, or say, 'Welcome aboard.'

"Even if they don't see, or choose to ignore me, that's fine. I've done my part in telling people that hey, you are who you are. Welcome on board. If their day becomes a bit better, I think I've done something right."

But what about progress? What about development? Doesn't he think about those? What makes him stay, even though he's had offers to leave?

He recognises the common narrative for people beginning their career is to chase a job that's well-paying.

"But at the same time, is that it? Is that what you want? Are you sure you can handle it? Because, in this race to meet societal expectations, sometimes we lose ourselves."

He's learnt how to deal with it by caring less about what people think of him, and to think more about himself. He confesses that there are times when societal expectations do get to him. For example, his friends were shocked that he moved from an office job to a blue-collar job like bus driving.

"But it doesn't matter. I'm a bit behind time, but I can still survive. I'm still contributing to society.

"Sometimes you wonder, what people say about chasing your education and chasing your career, is it worth it sometimes? Because it becomes chasing something to fulfil the norms.

"Why?

"If you have a goal, that's fine, I respect that. But if you're chasing just to be like everyone else, just for the sake of chasing, life becomes quite miserable."

I wonder what gave him the courage to leave a stable and secure office job. What would he say to those who want to leave, rather than stay? Many young people face the difficulty of admitting to themselves that their job isn't working out, and end up not leaving.

"Nothing is permanent. Even if you're forced to take on another job now, or [are] transiting to another career, it doesn't mean your life is over. Because you never know if it might bring you somewhere else, better!

"You might think, 'Oh, I'm changing to another career, especially another field I'm not familiar with. I'm screwed!' But change is what makes us grow. Sometimes just close your eyes, do it first and think about it later. Do first, think later."

Ce Xun bites into the first slice of his *kaya* (a coconut jam) toast, untouched since the start of the interview. It's probably cold by now.

But somehow this attitude of his, where he gives his all to what's asked of him, rather than his immediate physical needs, bears lessons for us.

Firstly, recognising that the biggest impediment to staying in a job, isn't others; it's *you*. It's your attitude. How you see the work. If a bus captain can see his work as cheering people up on their long commute home, surely, surely, we can see more of our "terrible" jobs.

Take some time to look beneath your work and ask: How might the end-client be impacted by my work?

Secondly, it's taking concrete actions to impact the end-client. Beyond the cliché of "make the most of what you have", Ce Xun took concrete actions to demonstrate that. Nodding to passengers. Putting a soft toy to cheer himself and other passengers up. Could you perhaps take time to see how you could make someone's day, such as a colleague's?

As we go along this chapter, we will talk through some mindsets you may not have consciously realised.

When many Gen Zs start working, it's difficult for them because we take mindsets that served us well in school and move that to work. These four mindsets end up affecting our work.

CUSTOMER MINDSET

At school, you're the customer. After all, you're paying (very) good money to get a degree, which should land you a good job. That's the hope.

Reality plays out quite differently.

You may take that perspective towards work. You feel that your bosses *should* offer you developmental opportunities. After all, in university, you had opportunity after opportunity emailed to you, straight into your inbox, and all you had to do was to click and apply.

That may happen in some workplaces, but not all.

That may come across to others as a sense of entitlement.

Changing that involves recognising that you're now taking money from your employer. You're expected to do a job in exchange for that money. Don't think like a customer. Think as a *contributor*.

ME-WORK MINDSET

Throughout school, the key performance indicator is *you*. It is how well you do at an exam, assignment, or paper you write.

Work is much different. It's not about "you". It's about "*us*". In a company, due to the sheer scale at which things are done, individual action may not count as much in moving the needle.

Coordinating and collaborating with different stakeholders enables more impactful work.

There are two distinct types of roles in a job. The team player, and the individual contributor. There are times when you are solely responsible for the outcome, such as when making a client presentation. Other times, e.g. planning an event, may involve more collaboration. Do you know which role you function best in?

Succeeding at work is about knowing when each role is needed, and moving smoothly across the scale from "me-work" to "we-work" (Fig. 5.1).

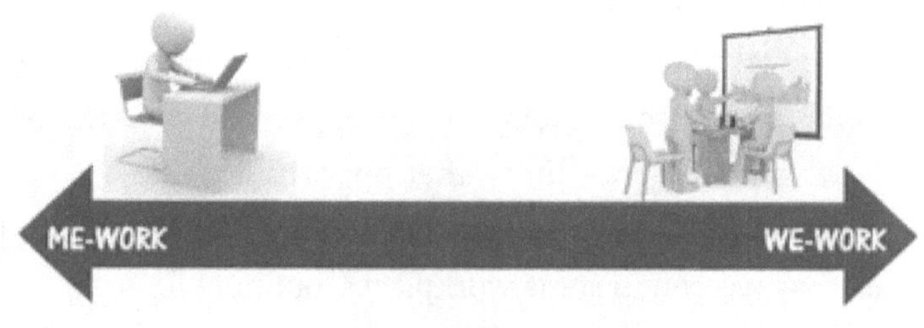

Fig. 5.1 Understand how each task requires different scales of me/we-work, and slide yourself along the continuum accordingly.

"I BELONG TO MYSELF" MINDSET

You're no longer representing yourself. At university, your assignments were labelled with your name. Now, it's your organisation's name at risk. You no longer represent yourself, but your organisation.

Even things you do in your own free time may turn its head to bite you. Thinking of posting a criticism online? Be careful. Even though you may say that it was posted in your own personal capacity, it's difficult to completely dissociate your professional role from the personal space you occupy. Employers may bring that to bear if they see something incongruent to the company's values.

"The private becomes political", especially when the private has now become public with the use of social media. Asking yourself whether you would want what you posted pasted on your mother's fridge is a good check against putting up something potentially damaging.

Representing yourself isn't about being true to yourself. Stephen Krempl (who I mentioned in Chapter 4) shared a common misconception young people have.

"Many of them make the mistake of thinking "I want to be true to myself; I want to be authentic'. They shoot themselves in the foot because nobody is 100% authentic. You can be authentic, but be authentic within your role.

"By role I mean, when you're a student in class, you act like a student in class. But if you are in a place of worship, you act differently. So how do you act in front of the senior people in your company? They don't realise that they are acting differently to different groups. But if you know how to act in front of senior leaders, you go up your organisation faster."

That's a fresh perspective. As young people accustomed to sharing personal details on social media, we may be tempted to bring that authenticity to interactions with our bosses. But as Grace, the SUTD lecturer that I highlighted in Chapter 2, explains, "Authenticity and transparency are not the same thing. There are different times for different qualities."

It's balancing between representing yourself, and the role you play.

"SMALL IS STUPID" MINDSET

In his book, *Not Everyone Gets a Trophy*, Bruce Tulgan observed many older bosses remarking that younger generations seemed to lack an appreciation of the value of graft, or working their way up. One manager told him, "They only want to do their best tasks."

You look at the small pieces of work assigned to you, and you may think, "This is so boring! Are you sure this is worth my time?"

After all, we've grown up in a world where we are constantly stimulated. Social media, Netflix, and the internet gave us constant variety. We may look at the small tasks assigned to us and feel they are too mundane. We want to do something new. Else, we quit.

But if you don't prove yourself trustworthy and reliable on the small things, why would managers entrust you with bigger tasks?

Knowing these four common mistakes, let's look at better ways to be retained by our work, finding interest, but also, the commitment when work gets boring.

KNOW WHAT YOUR JOB IS

Don't walk before you even crawl. In knowing what your job is, you need to know your boss's expectations of you, right from the start.

During my second year of work, I thought I knew my work well enough. I started commenting on the strategy and culture of the team, although I was the youngest. You can imagine how pompous it seemed for a 25-year-old, to be telling the leadership where we should be headed.

As exciting as that was, I was hauled back to reality. I was issued with a Performance Improvement Plan for not doing my basic job functions well. That's when I saw how important it was to know one's job description and do that well, before attempting anything unassigned.

In the opening conversation with your boss, take your job description along. Go through each line descriptor. Ask him what each descriptor looks like in your daily work. Then, ask him where it looks like you may be failing in each descriptor, and how you can help him be more assured of your competency.

This advice, from Assistant Professor Andrew Murphy at the University of Nottingham, is what enabled his students to pass placements where they had a high potential of failing. It's also what helps you consistently realign yourself with the expectations at work.

WORKPLACE RELATIONS

Often, the biggest barrier to sustaining your interest at work may be the relationships you have at work. Conflicts and "toxic" environments may leave you ready to throw in your resignation letter.

At some point, you'll have to deal with politics at work. There's no running away. But how?

Let's first understand what politics at work is, before thinking about resolutions.

Politics at work involves the human relationships in work. How do you navigate it, especially when you're at the bottom of the hierarchy, seemingly ready to be "eaten" by everyone else?

Grace, the SUTD lecturer, shares her wisdom.

"First and foremost, politics is inevitable. Because what is politics? Politics is, in essence, people having relationships with each other, and trying to influence each other to act in ways which you desire or for desired outcomes.

"Don't think of politics as something evil or bad or negative. Think about it neutrally. Like money. Money is neutral. It is the love of money that leads to greed and other vices.

"Politics is closely tied to interest. Everybody has self-interest whether they admit it or not. You need to learn to recognise these interests.

"I teach my students to begin by observing who hangs out with whom. And then you remember: A hangs out with B, then B plus C and D go out for lunch very often.

"They do this in organisations too, in case you think that organisations are not deliberate about networks. They map networks to figure out who to place in certain positions or teams. We call this organisational network analysis[1]."

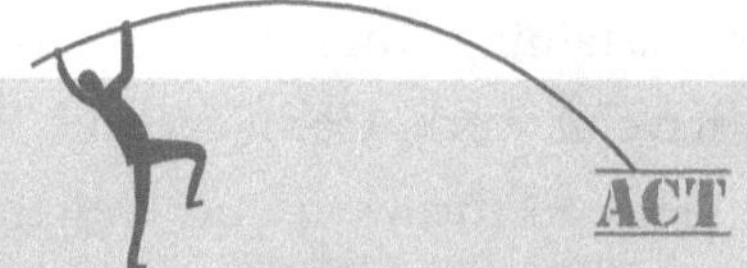

Draw out an organisational network map.
Who seems cosy with whom? Who doesn't seem to get along together? How do you relate to all these colleagues?

1 Cross, Rob, et al. "For an Agile Transformation, Choose the Right People." Harvard Business Review, Mar-Apr 2021, https://hbr.org/2021/03/for-an-agile-transformation-choose-the-right-people.

Grace goes on to say: "Contests in organisations usually occur over promotions and resources. When you compete for certain things, that's when various interests start kicking in. A natural outcome is for allies and coalitions to form.

"If you don't want to 'play', make sure you get out of the way. If you know that two factions are starting to form and you don't want to be part of it, then don't be seen with them.

"Whereas if you become a manager, and you have to go sort out the people who are fighting, what do you do? Same thing, you focus on those relationships.

"I often tell my students that if situations do not seem logical, it is likely to be political, or cultural."

Here's how *not* to do it.

Don't avoid it. In any organisation, you are bound to step into political minefields. You will find opposing factions, colleagues vying for power, and bosses who dislike each other. You will be drawn into the vortex of human relationships. Pretending it's not there is not the approach.

Dealing with politics at work is a common problem we hear from Gen Zs. After all, when relationships are mostly mediated through a screen on social media, and not liking someone is as easy to settle as "unfollowing" a person, you don't have to wade through the mess of real, human relationships and politics, in person.

What is a better way?

Firstly, acknowledge that there's going to be politics.

Secondly, build up alliances at work. You may say, "John, but this is not war … this is just work."

But allies help you feel less lonely at work. Whenever you suggest an idea at work, allies back you up, and speak for you. That can be very encouraging.

Thirdly, be political. I'm sorry. But I have to say this. You must be political if you want to survive in the workplace and succeed. Simply telling yourself that you're not going to play the game will not help. Rather than seeing politics as "bad", treat it neutrally.

Being political is about strategising and knowing where your alliances lie, and where your potential blockades are. As management guru Michael D. Watkins suggests in *Your Next Move*, this is about mapping out your network of key blockers and alliances, and those on the fence, so you know where your efforts would be most effective.

Let's say you want to bring a plan to fruition. There are some who support you, others who oppose you, and lastly, those who haven't decided.

Intentionally work on those who are on the fence. Doing this will ensure that you play the political game smartly, rather than pretending that it doesn't exist.

To find out more about the tricky issue of workplace relations, I spoke again to Grace, who teaches students how to understand the workplace better.

POLITICKING COMES WITH CHOICES: GRACE'S ADVICE

I'm meeting Grace at SUTD, the university where I studied for all of one day before deciding that I couldn't do it. Grace settles into the chair, leans back, and tells me that I have to stop her if she rambles on. I promise her that I won't walk out like how I did the first time.

What sparked her interest to do this?

"I observed that although we train students for work, we don't prepare them enough for the workplace. I heard stories from students returning from their internships 'traumatised' by their experience of the workplace, not knowing how to even process it.

What are the basic principles for better workplace relations? They must know themselves and what they are walking into."

Know Yourself

The first principle, as I found out, is to "know thyself".

Says Grace, "Knowing yourself is knowing your personality traits, your work preferences, and [who you are] at leisure. We put ourselves through many personality tests, but we never sit down to think about it.

"To us, it's obvious—such as tending to assume everyone thinks like us. But it comes to the fore when whoever you're working with, and whoever you're working for, is very different from you.

"Understand yourself enough to say that 'they' are different from [you], and learn to bridge that perceived gap between 'them' and 'us', especially when conflict arises."

I'm curious to know the concrete steps young adults can take to better understand themselves. After all, isn't understanding oneself a lifetime journey?

Grace tells me, "The first accessible thing you can do is to take personality tests. Survey yourself across several tests. Remember these tests are merely indications of your preferences. They are not 'truth'.

"Know your traits, your preferences, your work styles. Compare the results with what your friends say. Perhaps even check it with those who don't like you. You'll never know what you discover about yourself.

"Get the feedback so you get a well-balanced view of who you are, under work conditions and outside of work conditions. That gives you a sense of what work you prefer, what bosses you prefer, or the work styles you prefer. From there, you can gauge the types of workplaces you are better suited for.

"For example, if you find yourself not the sort to be compliant, don't work in hierarchical organisations. That would be logical, but not necessarily obvious."

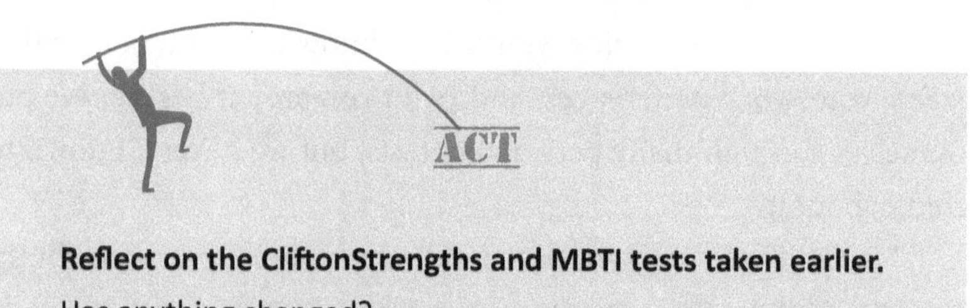

Reflect on the CliftonStrengths and MBTI tests taken earlier.
Has anything changed?

Know the Organisation

The second is knowing what you are walking into.

"For many students, the first full-time job carries with it hopes and aspirations for a bright future," says Grace. "It's easy to be lured by high pay, prestige, and benefits. You don't see the company for what it is. You see it for what you wish for. When it doesn't meet these grand expectations, you're frustrated and disappointed.

"I'd rather you pop your bubble of expectations before getting in. For example, companies like saying, 'We want your passion. We want you to love what you do.' Sounds wonderful, right?

"Until you ask the question: What business does a company have, wanting your passion? It's not for sale.

"But many are quite happy to say, 'Sure, fine. I sell you my everything', expecting care, concern, loyalty. And when they don't get those returns, things fall apart. They feel a sense of betrayal, anger, depression, burnout, and they don't know how to deal with it.

"Before you enter the workplace, be very clear: It is a contract you are signing as an adult, not a student. It is an employment contract. It is an exchange. A company is not your friend. The organisation does not exist to develop your personal aspirations, however much they may tell you that. You're there to work, and they're going to 'exploit' you, in essence. I'm saying this not to scare you but to help you see.

"The whole nature of a profit-driven company is that it is profit-driven. There are certain things it will demand of you. It is not there to make you feel good about yourself.[2]

"If you can see that much, it could temper all the 'grand aspirations', and take away some of the glamour. The hope is that when you go in there, you have a far more realistic perspective."

Being clear about your expectations of your employer can help you to know the expectations you're bringing and consciously decide whether there are some better worth leaving at home. The company doesn't owe you anything.

2 Harvey, David. *A Companion to Marx's Capital.* New York: Verso, 2010, pp 1-54.

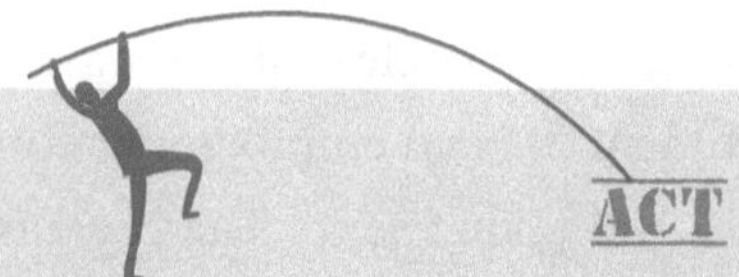

Write down a list of expectations you have of your employer, even the smallest details.

For example, you may write: boss gives me opportunities to stretch myself, etc.

Bad Bosses

Grace's Masters' thesis was an exploration of "bad bosses".

She states, "I don't think bosses start off trying to be 'bad'. We all try to be decent human beings. But a lot comes out from the assumptions or the perceptions we have about each other without understanding ourselves more. Or to understand the other person from where they are."

But what can young people do with perceived bad bosses, especially when they are at the bottom, with little influence, and needing the job to pay for their avocado toasts? (Okay, bad joke about avocado toasts; I know you don't eat them.)

Here's what Grace advises. "First and foremost, check out your own character and the other person's character.

"Character is the most consistent. If your boss is having a bad day, or a bad period in their life, give them space.

"Also, check yourself: Are you the one who's been unreasonable?

For example, a company is profit-driven. You cannot declare, 'Oh, you don't give me time off, you're making me stressed. I'm upset, and therefore, you're a bad boss.' The boss must also ensure things get done.

"It boils down to character. Is this 'bad' characteristic, consistent?

"Let's look at some theory. When you talk about bad leadership, there's a range of what's considered bad. You could be purely incompetent, which is a skills thing. Or be deceptive, which is a moral thing. There's a range of descriptors in between.[3]

"When somebody says, 'Joe is a bad boss,' they need to pin it down in all fairness. What exactly do you mean by bad? If this person is 'bad', is it because he is insensitive to my feelings? This is very different from this person is bad because he is manipulating me, or being violent, which is more serious.

"If you can at least define what you mean by 'bad', it helps you address it."

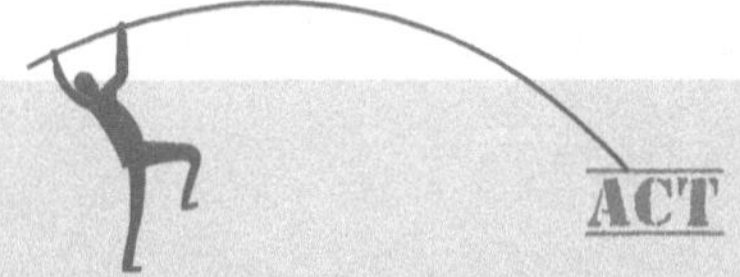

Draw two columns. On one side, put down behaviours that are 'okay'. On the other side, put down behaviours that are 'not okay'. This can help you better understand your triggers.

Grace goes on, "Let's say you have an incompetent boss, then go and find a competent one. Shift yourself within the organisation.

3 Kellerman, Barbara. *Bad Leadership: What It Is, How It Happens, Why It Matters.* Brighton, MA: Harvard Business School Press, 2004.

"If you think your boss is insensitive, have a conversation. Maybe it's a matter of traits. How he perceives you and how you perceive the other person.

"If it's a problem of character, then I will say, get out of the way. Because character is unlikely to change. If this person is generally mean and toxic to everybody all the time, get out of the way."

But not everyone can afford to quit. What then can they do?

"Theory, again, tells you [that] distance makes a difference," says Grace.

"There is the principle of proximity. If you don't want to be influenced by these toxic people, stay as physically far away from them. It can be as easy as getting a desk that's further away.

"If it's your boss, have somebody who can handle it in front of you, so you don't get bombarded all the time. Or instead of face-to-face, use email or text messages to create that distance."

Workplace Introverts

What if you don't like interacting with people? As author Susan Cain observed, today's workplace tends to favour extroverts. Extroverts can easily form networks, work in teams, and have great workplace relations with most people. What can introverts do?

"Introverts can build their own networks," says Grace. "It's just built differently. They build them in small groups. Small groups are okay for them. But build lots of little, small groups!"

"We have this theory called social network theory. You have people called 'nodes', or structural holes. Or in Hokkien parlance, your *lobangs.*

"It's always good to be in contact with a *lobang.* For an introvert, keep in touch with these people. If you only like talking to one person, then make it a *lobang*-person. They connect you to other people.

"Then you have strong and weak ties. Have a couple of strong ones. You can keep the rest weak, via LinkedIn or social media.

"I will say to the introvert, don't discount yourself. At some point, you can come out, have a couple of good friends. In the workplace, you don't have to be pals with everyone.

"But know who you should be in contact with for your work to get done. If you don't like networking, only go to those which have purpose.

"You don't have to be a social butterfly, but you need to be seen for people to remember you.

"The majority has shifted. There are more introverted, sensitive people now than we used to have. You're likely to find more people like you.

"Don't be afraid. Don't operate out of fear. It's better to move from a position of confidence. Because to me, fear is where you always back off from something.

"At some point, you'll back off to a point where you do nothing. You're paralysed and yet want something to change. Wherever you are, if you want something to change, move forward with a measure of courage. Not fear."

Somehow or rather, something she said sticks with me that night.

She was sharing her advice about what people should do when they find themselves stuck in jobs with toxic environments. I argued that young people 'cannot' afford to leave. She deliberately reframes that. "The [thing] is, it is not that you don't have a choice, it is that you don't like the consequences."

She reiterates. "You always have a choice. Learn to deal with the consequences like an adult."

It bears repeating. Many of us complain, without making the necessary choices that bring change. Complaining does little to change the situation. It is the choice you make. Even when you choose not to do anything, you're still making a choice.

In this chapter, we've looked at the intentionality that's required to sustain your engagement within a company. As Ce Xun showed, it's not just a job. But it's about daily actions that remind you why you do what you do. It's also about being clear on what you're doing, and where you best add value.

For tricky workplace relationships, it's recognising you have a choice in how you act, and accepting the consequences of your actions.

6

DEVELOPMENT

Welcome to the "valley of the suck".

I named it as such because it's the valley many employees go through the longer they work in a company. They find themselves familiar with how things are run.

That's when people think of moving to the next organisation.

But is it possible to constantly grow within an organisation?

That's when I spoke to Sascha, who started with Siemens, and has stayed with them for the last 15 years.

DEVELOPING YOURSELF AT A SINGLE COMPANY

In the process, he's risen to Vice-President in Siemens ASEAN. Sascha's story is uncommon, especially when we hear the stereotype of Gen Zs and millennials being serial job-hoppers.

How did he remain engaged? But more importantly, how did he progress so rapidly in this company?

After graduating from school, Sascha took a dual-study programme in Germany that exposed him to theoretical learning at university, whilst gathering practical experience in different commercial departments in Siemens. After working in blocks of six to eight weeks in a department, he returned to university to learn about the concepts.

In the past, when I spoke to Sascha about what he felt led him to his successful career, he credited luck. Today, I push him more for a deeper explanation.

He first credits the setting of a good foundation, with exposure to different parts of the organisation. "Besides studying, or going through internship programmes, I believe that when you start your career, it helps not to be too specialised on one specific skill or area of expertise. Instead, set yourself up broadly. Because if you start your career and you are too focused, your direction is already predetermined.

"If you start off widely, you get exposure to different parts of an organisation. You will have a fast learning curve and be able to cross-apply your learnt skills in different functions."

This confronts the conventional wisdom of going deep in a certain field.

Go Broad

Much of education today focuses on preparing specialists, channelling students towards a specific vocation, eventually culminating in a university degree in a specific knowledge vertical.

For example, you might notice the secondary school education exposing you to different subjects across geography, history, math, and science, is slowly limited to the arts or science stream in college.

Later in university, you pick *one* major, like history.

But building depth narrowly in a particular skill and knowledge may limit our abilities to solve "wicked" problems that require a breadth of knowledge and skills across different fields.

A range of skills and knowledge can help you think, before using the appropriate tool to solve the problem. As the T-Shaped Gen Z (Chapter 1) illustrated earlier, it's being multi-dextrous with different deeply-honed skills, whilst having a mental Swiss-Army knife of varying knowledge to incisively cut through problems.

There's the saying, "To a carpenter, everything looks like a nail". I will add to that saying. To a carpenter, everything looks like a nail that needs his hammer.

We should know many things but focus on doing the one thing.

Today, solving problems in your life may need different frames of reference and different tools of thinking. Those tools of thinking are called mental models.

Let's take for example a problem all of us will face: retirement planning. This is an example of a wicked problem.

As *Foresight: A Glossary* (published by the Centre for Strategic Futures and the Civil Service College, Singapore) defines, wicked problems are those with no simple solution because the precise nature of the problem cannot be defined. Ensuring one is adequately provided for during retirement is such an example because no one can accurately project what is going to happen in the future.

How you approach retirement planning requires different mental models, and the ability to *know* you're using different mental models. Deciding between the different insurers and investments, would already require you to employ different lenses. As David Epstein argues in his book, *Range*, we do not just need scientific spectacles to look at problems. But we also need a mental Swiss-army knife that allows you to tackle a problem with different tools in that Swiss-army knife.

How can you build depth, whilst simultaneously building *breadth*?

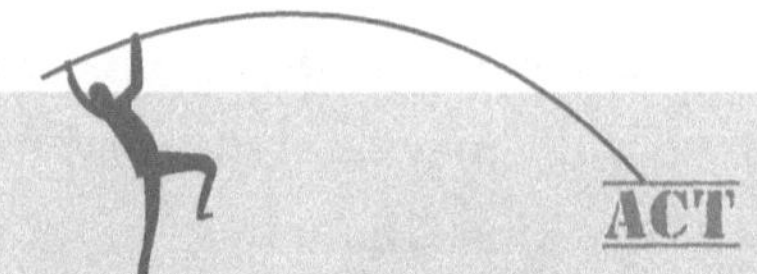

Read a book on mental models.
Start with Shane Parrish's books on Mental Models. Or you can start from fs.blog.

The simplest way, as Deddy (remember him from Chapter 1?) recommends, is to build life outside of school or work. Have a hobby that you devote considerable efforts to improve your skills on. Doing this has the added benefit of taking your mind off work.

Taking Sascha's advice may mean going for the generalist management associate job, rather than the highly specialised role.

Go Hard

Sascha's second piece of advice is common, but you don't hear it often. "In the first couple of years in the company or any new job, put in great effort. Work hard, stay humble and people will recognise it.

"Many today have high expectations towards a company and ask for more pay, faster progression, fast changes, and so on. It's important that you, of course, have your own requests.

"But at the same time, you must prove that you are contributing. Some people like to jump every two years or change companies frequently. My opinion is that whenever you take on a new role or responsibility, you have to make a proof point that you've contributed before moving on."

Chet, Senior Advisor to CapitaLand Development, shares a similar piece of advice, crediting her hard work for her ascent up the career ladder. She smiles as she looks back at those days.

"Those were fun times. Really crazy, but fun and engaging! I worked like mad. I would start at 7:00 a.m. and the earliest I ever left the office was 7:00 p.m.

"I was the only female in Facilities and Property Management. Even though I had no engineering experience, six months into the job, the General Manager made me the Building Manager for DBS Building! Can you believe it?

"Even though it was difficult, I kicked like hell, swam like hell … I never stopped kicking. You wouldn't believe the physical and mental stamina it took.

"I led a team of in-house technicians. Half of them were my father's age. I had to put some of them through disciplinary procedures, explain and justify to the Trade Union's Board of Inquiry. In those days it was different. The Union was very powerful! But I also learnt how to treat them right.

"I walked the talk. Even though we officially started at 8:30 a.m., I was on-site by 7:00 a.m. I would be there six days a week. Even though I was supposed to enjoy every third Saturday off, I would come back to catch up on the paperwork. I had to manually go through all the petty cash claims, time-off claims, medical certificates, and overtime claims, and sort them into different piles. For those that I had queries, I would follow up on Monday and resolve them.

"Even though I had no engineering background, I was very young and determined. My team eventually respected me. They initially doubted me because they thought I had little know-how for the job. They were like, 'Can Chet do the job?'"

Some say that Gen Zs have grown soft and lazy. It's time to prove them wrong.

Flex

Sascha's last advice is to be flexible.

"If you are flexible in terms of a potential next step—which country, which function, which area of responsibility—you have much more options. And if an opportunity comes, grab it!

"There is never a 'good timing', because your personal life might have to take a step back. But looking at change as a growth opportunity, rather than a threat, helps you progress in your personal and professional life.

"On the contrary, if you're very focused and say, 'This is exactly what I want to do next,' that may not work.

"Looking at the beginning of my career, I would have never thought of the steps which led me to where I am today. I worked for different business units in various roles in three different countries. I didn't plan my career. I was flexible and grabbed opportunities when they came up.

"If you think an opportunity is interesting and worth going for, go for it. Then, you have to follow it through, make your contribution.

"Especially in today's world, we need to stay vigilant. Life typically does not go as planned. Plans change and we need to be flexible enough to adapt."

Sascha explains that at Siemens, because of the wide diversity of business units they have, changing between business units can feel like working for a different company. Along with changing responsibilities in different countries, this has helped him to find new challenges and new things to learn.

GROW INTO ROLES

But I'm keen to know how Sascha found such a good fit between the jobs he had, and his skill sets. How did he find roles where he excelled in? I point out that some go through life never truly finding what they are good at.

"Good point. That takes time. It's not easy to see and reflect on yourself.

"Firstly, I would not try to go for a position where I think my skill set fits. Of course, you're required to fulfil certain criteria, like a degree, to qualify for a job.

"Instead of looking at where my skill set fits best, I would look for something where I'm interested in and excited about. The skill set is secondary because you can learn skills.

"If you are excited about a position or job or function or company, this motivates you and brings you energy. It's important to do something you like, because if you don't, then after a short time, you'll quit, or it will not be successful. Because you don't put in all your efforts.

"Find out what you are interested in, what drives you, rather than what fits your skill set. You will develop your skills along the way."

Hearing Sascha's advice reminds us of three things to develop in ourselves at the company. Firstly, grow in a range of skills, understanding different business functions. Then, be flexible, seizing opportunities that appear. Lastly, find something you're interested in.

That is difficult to hear.

Throughout this book, I've argued that digging deep into your skill is the difference separating you from the average Joe.

But Sascha recognises that if you're not excited about a project, however great you are at the work makes no difference.

Find work that excites you. Doing that doesn't require you to sacrifice interest or skill. You can engage in both.

But in our first or second jobs, we often don't have clear, concrete steps we can take to ascend the career ladder. Questions like:

- When is it time to move?
- When should you stay?
- How do you grow at a job?

These are questions we sought advice from Chet, who ascended the ranks in the construction industry, against all odds.

ACHIEVE VELOCITY, NOT SPEED

I'm seated across the table from Chet, who officially retired in 2021. Her last role before retiring was Senior Vice President in CapitaLand, responsible for Retail Innovations, Strategic Partnership for mixed-use developments and iconic projects, mentoring and training colleagues across the region. She still serves as a consultant and Senior Advisor to CapitaLand Development and its portfolio of iconic projects.

I asked her how she's been so successful in her career. She immediately qualifies her success.

"I wouldn't say I'm successful. I've never been in the C-suite.

"I never wanted to be in the C-suite. In fact, I once told my Board that if I ever get into the C-suite, I only want to be the CFO. When the CFO in the meeting heard this, he immediately sat up and adjusted himself. He was uneasy and thought I was coming for his job!

Then I giggled and gleefully told them, 'I want to be the Chief Fun Officer!'"

She laughs.

Define Your Success

Chet continues, "It's not good to define a certain view of success for young people, to lock them into a certain paradigm. For me, it's better to have an open-ended perspective of success. There's different focus of success for different phases of our lives. For my two young grandchildren, success is having a nice swim to complete the length of the pool! Success is not a destination. It's a journey of possibilities!"

From Chet, the mindset we hold in our careers shouldn't be of a fixed idea of success, but rather, having a variety of ideas about what success means. As Daniel Wong shared in *The Happy Student*, defining your own success is writing down actions you will take, rather than outcomes you will achieve. You may never control the outcomes you get. But you can always control the actions you take.

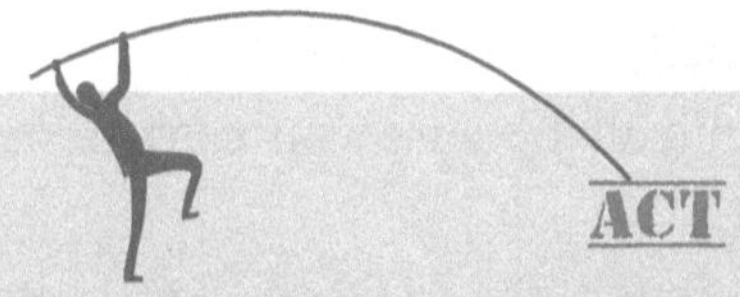

How would you define your own success?
For example, my definition of success is: Showing up daily to create, whether I like it or not.

Chet believes that climbing in one's career starts from a firm foundation of values. "I started in 1978 as a quantity surveyor with a small family-owned company. My boss taught me so much about being a good human being, upholding good Chinese values such as 义气 (loyalty).

"In quantity surveying, you're supposed to look at the progress of work done, and materials delivered to site and then agree on their values with the respective subcontractors and suppliers.

"I remembered that his four sons would urge me to go to their father to report their deemed market values. They were concerned that their father would always insist on giving his 'fair' valuation.

"If he knew that a supplier or subcontractor was in financial trouble, he would willingly overpay him to tide them over. If another had lost money on horse racing over the weekend, he would also assist by giving more! So naturally I was always caught between the father and his sons!"

Hearing this, I'm curious. What made her so special that this boss took time to teach her the tricks of the trade?

"John, you've talked to me for what … almost an hour? What you see is what you get. I've shared with you everything I know. I don't need to lie because you end up having endless lies to cover earlier lies. When you lie, especially when you get older or even have dementia, it becomes very difficult because you can't remember what you said in the past."

Honesty and loyalty are two values Chet prizes. It's not about following her values, but *knowing* your own values.

When To Move

From that family business, she wanted to experience another aspect of the industry. She wanted to join the government or a top developer because she saw them as being top of the "food chain", approving land use and city planning, and being the ultimate paymasters for many development projects. In 1980, she applied for both the Property Management Division of DBS, as well as the government. She received the government's offer first and signed their letter of appointment.

However, she changed her mind subsequently and wanted to experience the commercial world when DBS's offer came along.

There was a snag. If she wanted to change her decision, she had to pay a compensation to the civil service, comprising three months of notice in-lieu, although she had yet to start work with them. She went to the HR of the government agency to ask for a discretionary waiver. They did not agree. She asked if she could speak to the gentleman who chaired the panel for her job interview. "I explained the situation. And he said, 'Okay, I will approve this for you.'"

She went on to join DBS Property Management Division.

Chet's story shows two things. Firstly, developing oneself at a company doesn't always necessitate *staying* in one company.

Here, it's difficult to give a generic principle such as "always move to a larger firm". Instead, move to what you need. Even though Chet was performing well at her company, she wanted to experience something different.

Secondly, it's okay to change one's mind along the way. Not every decision made would be right. What's important is to acknowledge when one wants a change, and make that change happen. Often, we stay stuck and wait for the job to change for the better, rather than taking action ourselves. If you need a bigger pay cheque, move. Not every move needs to be developmental.

As Bruce Tulgan explained in *Not Everyone Gets a Trophy*, there are different jobs for different seasons in life (Table 6.1, overleaf). there are times when we just need an easy job, where it's not too challenging. You may need to sort out other things in life, such as marriage.

Type of Job	What This is
Safe harbour job	Stable job and you're there mainly to collect your pay cheque
Weigh station job	You're at a point where you're weighing your options and figuring what you want to do next
Peer group job	Your friends/colleagues are the main reason why you stay
Big gamble job	You see this as an opportunity to work like crazy for a period with the chance of a big pay-off at the end
Needle in a haystack job	You're looking for a job that meets a particular or unique need or one that requires a special schedule/skill/task
Passion job	You work in a job that aligns with your interests and priorities even if you think the pay may not be that great
Self-building job	You're looking for an opportunity to make an impact while building yourself up with your own resources

Table 6.1   Different jobs for different times of your life as espoused by Bruce Tulgan.

Life's development doesn't only need to come *within* a job. It can come from outside the job, such as in romantic relationships. What's vital though, is that your job serves your life's development. Take a step back from "career" development and look at your *life's* development.

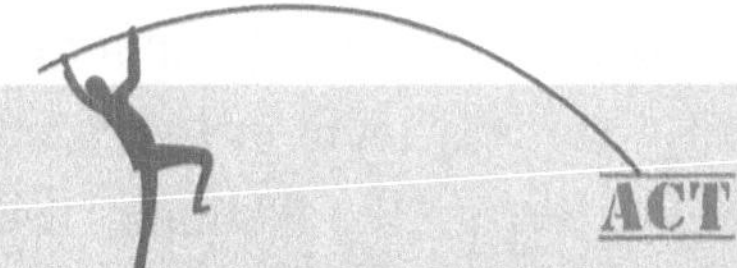

Try asking yourself: What are your priorities right now? What do you need from a job at this moment to serve your life's priorities?

Teach Others

"My bosses sent me for many overseas study trips and training," says Chet. "After each overseas stint, I took time to train my team, to practise with them, to share with them. The moment I train my staff, things change!

"I always give them everything. You know the Chinese saying about only imparting 80% of kung fu so the student will not surpass the master?

"I don't believe that. I give everything I know to my staff.

"Always share your learning journey. Don't be selfish. Teach everything.

"Give everything."

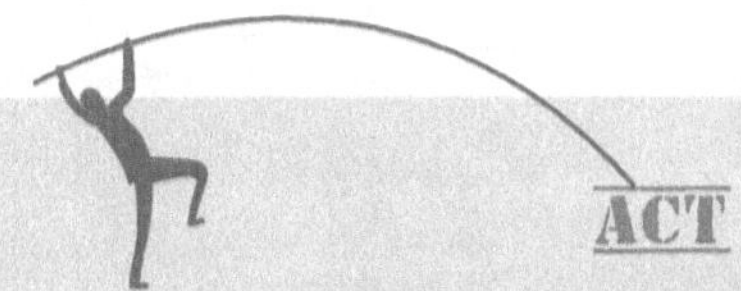

Are there new interns in your team that you can teach?

Gently taking people under your wing, showing them something simple like how to use the photocopier may seem insignificant, but it also reminds you of what you've learnt. The National Training Laboratories in Maine found that teaching others helped one to retain an average of 90% of the information. In comparison, reading was only found to help one retain 10% of information!

Give Everything

"Give everything". It bears repeating. In this day and age, how many of us can say that we are giving 100% to our jobs?

Today, having a side hustle, or running a pet project, is common. But looking at the story of Chet, it's a story of 100% commitment. Nothing less than her best. A heart to make the best of every opportunity presented. Even when she wasn't ready, she threw herself into the deep end and rapidly learnt the ropes. Perhaps that's the thing we miss in our jobs—100% commitment.

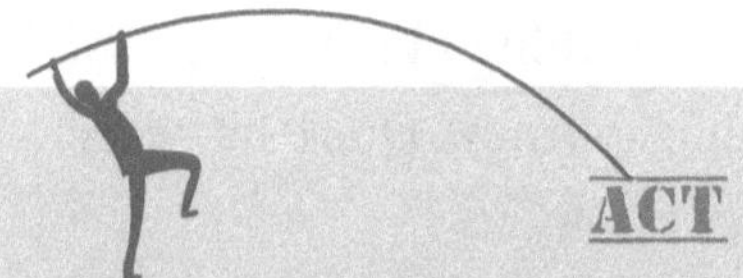

Today, take time and map out all the projects you have in your life.

Ask yourself:
- How much effort are you putting into your job?
- Is your job your priority, or just another thing you're doing?

Chet didn't spread herself thinly. She wasn't doing many different projects in her free time. She only focused on what she loves—God, her family, and her job.

Somehow that advice seems prescient today. Even when there're so many opportunities available and we can do anything, that doesn't mean we should do everything. Maybe it's time to stop pining after the things you don't have.

Instead, return to the basics of making the most of who you are, where you are and what you have. Do everything diligently. Give *everything* you've got, to what you've got.

Total commitment.

But as we grow in our work, we will face poor bosses or colleagues that impede our development. What do we do?

YOU SUCK!: ARIEL'S WORKPLACE STRUGGLE

Ariel (remember her from the Preface?) graduated from a British university under an overseas scholarship. As an academic high achiever, she was keen to make the most of her first full-time job. After returning from England to her home country, she started work the next week.

Even though this was her first job, she was expected to oversee the creation of a new quality assurance function within the company. Despite having no work experience, she was made a manager.

With no supervisors she could learn from, and few colleagues who could guide her, she felt thrown in the deep sea, without a float. She struggled.

Week after week, she would cry as her boss shouted at her, and asked questions like, "Why am I even paying you?"

There were other times when her boss said her work "sucked".

She also faced little help from her colleagues. Being the youngest, her colleagues did not listen when she gave them instructions.

After all, they wondered why they should when she was the least experienced amongst them. There were other times when her colleagues said she didn't deserve the pay she was getting.

Working in quality assurance, and when preparing for an audit, she woke at 6:00 a.m. every day to go to work, and only left the office at 10:00 p.m. to return home. She did this from Monday to Saturday, for an entire month.

Despite this, she helped her company to get the prestigious BRC (Brand Reputation through Compliance) certification, an infamously difficult audit process in the food industry.

As she reflects on this time, she smiles. It's clear that she's grown much since the time she started. Looking back, how would she advise others in similar positions, where they are under tremendous pressure and struggling to see how to grow in their current company?

Being Bad is Okay

The first? It's okay to suck at your job.

As Ariel says, "It's not the end of the world if you suck at your job. We don't need to be perfect in everything."

But how did she manage to have this mindset shift, especially after doing so well at university?

She smiles. "I'm a perfectionist. When I started to work, I thought, 'I need to be the best, I need to give my all.' It was very difficult to accept that I'm not good.

"But, it's a good thing that you're not good at this job. Now you know that and you can focus on something else that you might be good at.

"Remind yourself that there're many options. You don't know unless you try."

When we have bad experiences at jobs, we don't realise we can quit. We don't have to stay there. We can take lessons from the job and move on. As one mentor once said, "Treat each job as a learning experience and don't take it personally."

There's Only You

The second piece of advice? You are the only "you".

"In the end," says Ariel, "Even though you're working so hard for the company, you're making someone else richer and richer. Like the CEO or the management team. They don't even know you! You're just a small tool that can be easily replaced by somebody else.

"But you're the only you for your family and friends. If something happened to you, they cannot replace you with someone else. Give 100% to your work during working hours. After that, take your time to enjoy life."

This mental mindset is vital in preserving boundaries between work and home. Simple steps include:

- Removing the email app on your phone;
- Separating work and personal phone numbers; and
- Not checking email/instant messaging after work hours.

These can ensure that you're working hard at work, and resting hard(er) when at home.

The last piece of advice?

"The most valuable lesson is that I have many other aspects of my life to celebrate. Maybe your boss might make you feel guilty about the task you cannot achieve. Remind yourself that it's not the end of the world. You might fall into these bad relationships at work, and find yourself saying to yourself, 'You're not good enough. You cannot get better.'

"Speak to your friends, or your family about your problem. Don't feel like you need to face work on our own. Talk to someone who loves you. Don't get into those traps because honestly, they don't care.

"Why listen to someone who doesn't care about you? Seek help."

Looking back at those dark moments, what kept Ariel going?

"What made me keep going is that, even though it's difficult and dark, I need that moment, I need that experience to grow as a person.

"And also, I need some money …"

At this, we laugh. It's remarkable that despite all that she's gone through, Ariel can still joke. She ends with this final advice.

"I had a friend who told me to think about a funny moment when people were being mean. So, I imagined myself detaching from the situation, and looking at my boss hopping mad, shouting and screaming. I laughed to myself because she was being so dramatic.

"Think about funny things even when that person is being mean. Life doesn't have to be so serious."

In your first job, there are times where you find yourself being treated less well than you expected. For others, you may struggle with understanding how to make the best of the company to grow.

But Ariel shows us that focusing on herself, and seeking help from people who loved her, kept her going.

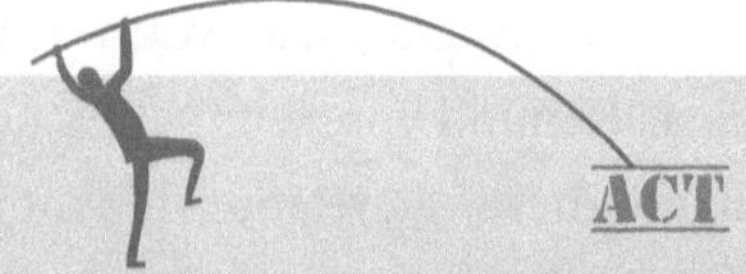

Make a list of people you can call or message whenever you need help.

DO MORE THINGS

Chet's story reveals a myth we may have towards work—that doing more things may bring us further in work.

Not so. It's doing the *right* things, not everything. In Morten Hansen's study of 5,000 employees, he found that the best focused on the biggest drivers of value. Rather than giving themselves to-do lists, they created to-*add* lists.

They understood what their biggest drivers of value were in the work they did. Not all work is created equal. Replying an "okay" in an email may not be as important as preparing an important pitch for a potential client.

Therefore, knowing where your biggest value-add lies is important. Why don't we do this? Because it's easier to do the shallow work of replying to a message, rather than sitting down to think, "Am I doing this to look busy? "

This question, asked by Tim Ferriss in his book, *The Four-Hour Work Week*, forces you to think about whether you are working, or pretending to work. Sometimes, we may be caught in busy work, rather than *good* work. Knowing the difference, moves you towards the things that drive value.

But knowing this is not enough. How do you develop yourself in the company you're at, making the most of the opportunities that are given to you?

DEVELOPING WITH SOFT SKILLS

Ultimately, developing yourself in a company seems less about the technical skills, but more the soft skills of interacting with others.

Amidst all the hiring for technical competencies today, it bears noting that amongst career luminaries, they still believe in the power of soft skills like attitude, teamwork, and communication.

For Dr Candice Chee of MentorsHub, she often chooses the person with the better attitude over the person who may be very smart. "No employer wants someone who's smart and arrogant, and thinks he knows everything. They would rather hire someone who's teachable, who's got a good attitude. Attitude trumps aptitude, any day."

Jay Ng, the CEO of Weshine, agrees. He observes that even in-demand computer engineering graduates may find themselves priced out of the market, compared to cheaper labour from abroad.

Knowing this, how can young graduates differentiate themselves?

"Soft skills," he replies. "I've met many graduates in the industry, and they are not doing front-end developer jobs. They are doing tech sales, for example. These soft skills cannot be outsourced."

Soft skills may not seem that important. After all, how important can they be if most work occurs over the digital world today, and you may hardly meet your colleague in person?

But soft skills can be the mediating gel between you and a difficult colleague. It can make work smoother.

Make no mistake. Soft skills can be built. It's being intentional about building it, rather than leaving it to chance.

Be Purposeful

Know where you're lacking.

There are three aspects of soft skills, listed in Bruce Tulgan's book, *Bridging the Soft Skills Gap*, of which there are many (Fig. 6.1).

- Followership

  Do I know how to follow people and the context of the organisation I'm at?
- Critical thinking

  Do I know how to think, rather than just googling the answer?
- Professionalism

  Am I professional with my work?

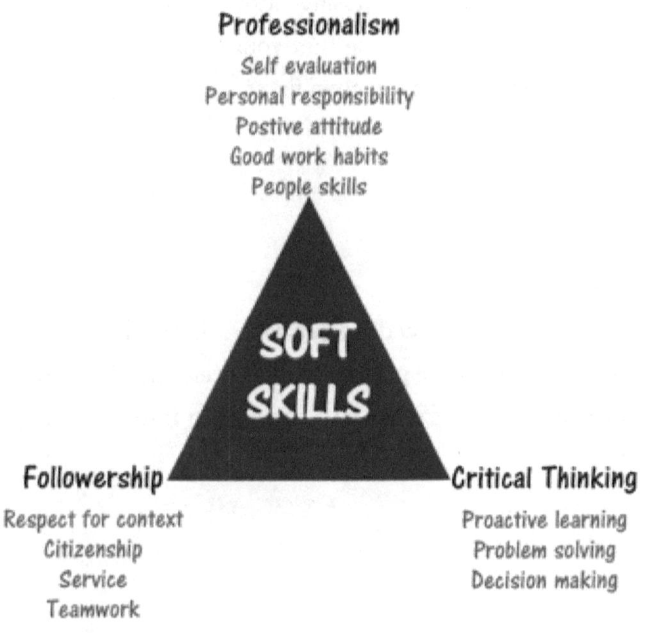

Fig. 6.1 Some examples of the soft skills that you build up to bridge the gap.

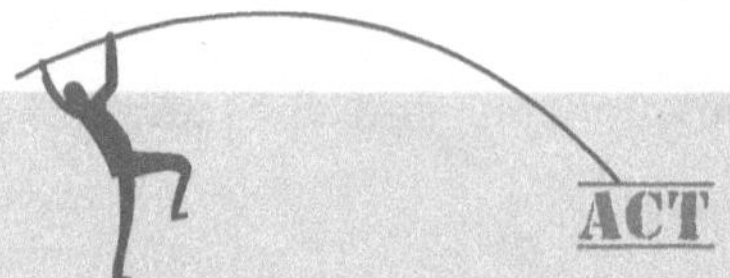

Take the time to go through Tulgan's list of soft skills.

Check the ones that you don't feel you're as good as.

Weekly, focus on small, concrete actions that will move you towards a greater competency on the line item listed above. For example, if you lack a positive attitude, you may focus on the small action of ensuring that your facial expressions are soft and welcoming, rather than fierce and scary.

Be Practising

Soft skills are a muscle, needing practice. That's why after knowing your gaps, come up with a plan to work better with them. In Fig. 6.2, you can see a sample of what you can use to intentionally practise your soft skills.

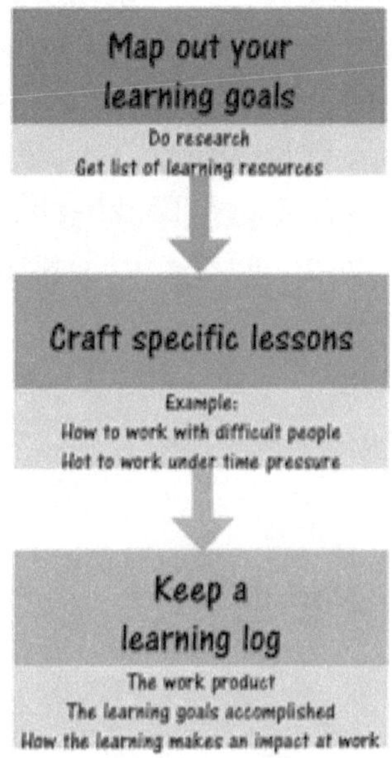

Fig. 6.2 According to Bruce Tulgan in *27 Challenges Managers Face,* these are some areas in which you can practise your soft skills.

Be Processing

Lastly, reflect on your journey. Don't leave it to chance. Instead, adjust along the way. It's not the plan that matters.

It's the *planning* that makes the difference. It's the adjustment along the way that builds a better self, with better soft skills.

In August 2021, I finished my Performance Improvement Plan. Directors, supervisors, and HR sat around a Zoom meeting talking through the pointers I'd reached. There were no celebrations. I didn't feel a great sense of success. As much as it felt like a weight off my shoulders, I hadn't developed much.

If anything, I had gotten worse.

Everyone commented on how I grew quieter over the course of the six months. Reflecting, I saw how fear had driven me to shut up. Fear drove me to tell myself that there was no point in sharing ideas. The wider issues of teamwork, people skills, and a positive work attitude were not developed. Looking back, I failed to develop because I simply wanted to get the process over and done with. I didn't reflect throughout.

Expecting others to do something that would improve you, is hopeful. It may not happen though.

It's in your hands.

It's your work.

It's time for you to work those changes out.

7

SEPARATION

When should you leave your job? How do you leave?

Movies glamourise the employee who yells, "I QUIT!" in his boss's face before walking out. But it's not that dramatic.

Before speaking about separation, there are a few myths to address.

LEAVING MAKES THINGS BETTER

If you're bullied, abused or not having a good time at your workplace, leaving can make things better. But thinking it will *always* do so is a myth.

There are times when leaving will not solve things. For example, if you're emotionally abused by your boss, leaving may remove the stress, but it may not solve the deeper emotional trauma you've experienced. Nor does it mean you've grown in addressing conflict with others.

Leaving also does not necessarily change the outlook of things. In fact, it could introduce greater pressures into your life, such as facing continual rejections, needing to ask for money from your parents, and watching your bank account dwindle daily.

You do need considerable mental resilience and belief in yourself to make things better. Leaving is the first step, but it's not the *final* step. Often, the transformation towards an engaging career only starts *during* the search. It's during this search—what I term the "wilderness"—that you begin to draw comfort from being in the wild.

LEAVING FOR SOMETHING DIFFERENT

If you've had a bad experience in your first job, leaving for something different can be hard to secure. Especially in your early career. Employers who look at the limited experience on your CV might find it difficult to try you in a different role, compared to someone with more relevant experience or qualifications.

That's why the Slide-Step Framework encourages you to establish that personal connection with someone, and help them informally, before they give you a chance. This beats toiling up the mountain of HR processes, which may get you nowhere.

Knowing when to leave your job is more an art, than a science. For Gen Zs, we've been known as the job-hopping generation.

There isn't a problem with that. On hindsight, as I reflect on my journey and interviewed people who left their jobs, three principles emerged as useful anchors for the wilderness.

KNOW WHY YOU'RE LEAVING

Separating from a job is easy.

Type an email, say you're resigning, thank them, and that's it. For those of you who've never done it before, it's *that* simple. Of course, it's helpful to tell your boss that you're leaving and that you're not planning to continue. But as long as you serve your notice, leaving is part and parcel of work.

When I first typed out *the* resignation letter, I was scared. I thought this was the be-all and end-all.

After sending, there was barely a ripple. No dramatic walking into the boss's office, throwing my resignation letter on his table, before walking out. No screaming matches.

Only a boring email, and a simple acknowledgement from the boss. That's all.

But to reach that point where you're willing to write that email will take time. That's what we are going to explore today.

The list of reasons why one takes (and stays in) a job, from Bruce Tulgan's *Not Everyone Gets a Trophy* is revisited here again.

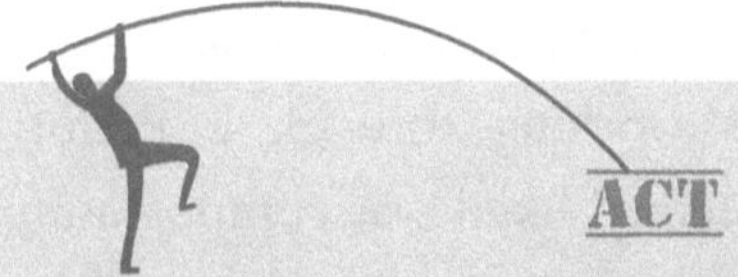

Ask yourself why you started the job you're currently in, and why that reason no longer works today.
(You can refer to Table 6.1 in Chapter 6 for a list of some of the reasons why we work.)

Ideally, in deciding to leave, both push and pull factors should be explored. Push factors are those causing you to leave your current job. Pull factors are those that attract you to your next position.

What's the right answer to when you should leave?

Here in Singapore, we love our model answers.

The model answer is the last, where you find a job that's self-building. You want to grow your employer's work, *with* your employer, whilst doing work that fits you.

Unfortunately, an imperfect world demands a more nuanced answer. Knowing whether to stay or leave is tough.

Leave, when what the job brings no longer matches with what *you* want to do, and what you need.

OSCILLATING

One question though. How do you decide when to leave? The constant oscillation between staying or going may tear you apart. What's particularly difficult is the 'what-if', the feeling that if you made the wrong move, the other move may have turned out much better.

A Personal Story of Oscillation

During my first job, a great offer came to work with a known people developer. It was with a company with great ambition.

But at that time, I was working through a Performance Improvement Plan. Leaving seemed like I was running away from improving the issues raised.

I oscillated and swung between point to point. I was given a week to decide. Up till the final hour, I had not decided. There were days when I woke up and thought that I should go, because it was a good move for my career.

There were other times when I felt the project management skills required were not ones I had. I called mentors. I wrote a pros and cons list. I even took time to work through career assessments, exploring where my passion and strengths lay.

The night I was supposed to send my decision, I went down to the park to walk. I hoped a walk would clear my head and give me time to reflect on my previous experiences. I made up my mind to stay. But as I showered, I suddenly thought of all the reasons I should go.

Pardon me. This was my first experience of a career move and I had no anchors of where I was, what I wanted do, and no concrete handles on deciding.

I recounted an incident earlier that day. I was visiting a rental flat, playing with the children of the family I was helping. The child was climbing over my head.

Immediately, I knew an indirect role wouldn't afford me such a luxury. It would be difficult to envision the possibility of this in my new role, where there was more paper pushing than people work. That night at 11:58 p.m., I told the employer I wasn't accepting their offer.

This seemed like happy ever after.

Cue John succeeding with a revitalised commitment to his workplace, gaining accolades, working better with teammates, and making a difference.

Nope. Not even close.

In the first week after rejecting the offer, I spent more time with my colleagues. I went out for lunch with them, spent time focused on my work … but when the first difficulty came, I thought, "Why didn't I take the job that came?"

After my 91st job application, that decision seems all the more stupid.

So, I thought: Maybe I should speak to someone about how we can decide better.

Oscillating is Part of Life: Adeline's Story

That's where Adeline comes in. Adeline is a seasoned marketer who has transited across different industries like banking, telecommunications, and fintech.

Her first decision was choosing between an established bank and a local start-up telco. "At that time, I was thinking how I could establish myself. At a bank, there were many seasoned marketers. But at a local start-up, I could be given more opportunity to establish myself.

"Always, whenever I look at a career decision, I look at my chance of success. At the local start-up, I had the chance to increase my visibility."

If you look at a potential job, ask yourself how confident you are of bringing something different. Playing in an overcrowded field, where everyone is jostling to get in, may not be best for your career. Instead, go to where you will be valued. Being a big fish in a small pond seems better.

When do you stay, or leave?

"Play to your strengths," says Adeline. "The Gallup CliftonStrengths helped me see that I was better in connecting the dots. Knowing your strengths is very important.

"Over the years, I've learnt to ride the wave. For example, when I returned to banking, it wasn't in consumer credit. I moved into the trend in wealth management.

"I always suggest to my mentees that they need to network, speaking to industry professionals to understand the trends."

That strikes me. It's not about being in the right place, but *getting* to the right place. This adage—network, network—keeps popping up, as if it were some golden rule.

Why bother? After all, who's got the time to network when there's so much to do?

But it seems the network doesn't only help you find work in current industries, but also figure out where to move to *next*. It's understanding the trends, so you catch the next wave.

What if leaving doesn't solve problems, but creates new ones?

"I always advise young people that if they are not enjoying their jobs, it's better to leave quickly." Adeline's "action-bias", where she encourages one to leave unhappy work, without getting stuck in worry, pushes one to differentiate between one's circle of control, circle of influence, and circle of awareness. This concept, from Stephen Covey, focuses us on fixing the present, without losing ourselves in unforeseen futures.

Her parting advice to young people?

"Build a career lattice," she says. "Don't just climb the corporate ladder."

A career *lattice*? That's new. I've heard of career ladders and corporate ladders. But a lattice?

Adeline explains. "It's having new skill sets, that layer one on top of the other. At the start of your career, build technical competencies. But as you move up, you should build lateral skill sets."

She explains with an analogy of burger, fries, and ice cream. The burger is your core skill set. The fries are the additional, lateral skills that distinguish you from the rest. The ice cream is the icing on the cake. It's the one that makes you special.

Hearing from Adeline gives me a better handle on what I could have done when faced with that situation earlier in my career. Ask yourself the following questions:

- What is my strength?
- Does this job suit my strength?
- Is the new role riding on a new trend, or wave?
- What stage of life am I at? What are my needs? Do I need a job to support dependants, or do I need a job for self-actualisation, to fulfil a desire for fulfilment?

Knowing this helps us to move into addressing the final question in deciding whether to stay or leave what you've been trained for.

CHANGING FIELDS IS OKAY: CHIEN PING'S STORY

Changing fields completely can seem crazy. But Chien Ping did it.

By many accounts, Chien Ping has succeeded. Today, he is the Director of People, Culture and Sustainability at WhiteCoat Global. But it wasn't the way his career started.

He graduated with a degree in civil engineering before training as a teacher. For three years, he worked as a teacher. But he didn't feel like he was properly managed or looked after.

His story is inspiring because you would think that success starts early. You would think that it starts with the "right" degree, the "right" job after university, and a steady progression up the ranks. But that's not Chien Ping's story.

How did he find the courage to leave a safe and secure job like teaching, to explore something entirely different?

"I always get asked that," he chuckles. "Number one, there's this thing called happenstance theory. Basically, just try it.

"Young people need to adapt. They need to have this mental model, of being willing to try new things. But at the same time, don't keep doing it.

"When you've reached a certain age, you ought to have tried enough to know where you want to go.

"Once you graduate, don't be fearful of trying multiple jobs. Don't think, 'I must go into a civil service job or MNC.' And don't think of putting off a job, because of the money or the brand.

"But look at what kind of jobs you want to try. What exposure do you want?

"Don't go into the job expecting it to be giving to you. Know what you want out of it. Don't go to a job waiting for things to happen. Take charge and be accountable for your own development."

Chien Ping shares a good timeline to try new jobs.

"In the first four to five years of graduation before turning 30, try. You have youth on your side. You can share with the recruiter that you've tried all these different jobs, and this is where I want to go. It will be more convincing, not only to the interviewer, but to yourself.

"The age of 30 to 35 is when you deepen your skill sets. And from 35 onwards, you should be finding that broad spectrum of leadership opportunity where you spend your last few years.

"But before that, it is the golden opportunity to be trying new things. Don't be afraid of taking risk."

But what about those who face the fear of "sunk costs"? They have spent four years studying at university (and a lot of money). To admit that this may not be what they like or are best at is difficult.

Chien Ping agrees. "What we learn in school is not about the product. It's about the process. What we trained in the four years of our degree is the way we think. It's not so much about finding a job in what you graduated in. It's how you use that experience. You need that transference of skills into other roles."

Chien Ping's advice about trying and failing, and learning from each successive experience is a common thread behind the advice of many others. Rather than seeing one's career as a *ladder*, where one is climbing upwards, people like Chien Ping has advocated seeing one's career as *learning*, where one learns more about oneself, and what one likes or doesn't like.

Most importantly, the distinguishing factor between a job and a career, is *that they can integrate what they do at work into what they achieve in life.*

That it no longer becomes a work-life balance, but as Chien Ping calls it, a work-life *integration.*

We know though that, in reality, moving from industry to industry is not as easy. Establishing a reputation is vital if you want to be headhunted for a bigger role. That's where reputation management comes in.

REPUTATION MANAGEMENT: ALAN STEVEN'S ADVICE

Knowing the importance of reputation, especially in advancing one's job, led me to speak to Alan Stevens, a reputation management expert.

Alan's first reminder? *Everyone* has a reputation. It's why employers insist on reference checks and why they ask you to send referees who can attest to the work you've done.

Early in one's career, the mistake young people often make, as Alan tells me, is thinking that they don't have that *big* a reputation. After all, they are not famous superstars! Young people end up posting pictures of a wild night out, or rude comments. They think reputation doesn't matter.

Alan begs to differ. He shares the story of the South African woman who posted something rude on Twitter, before hopping onto a plane from the US to South Africa. When she landed, she found reporters wanting to speak to her, her name splashed on the newspapers, and that she had lost her job. *Everyone* has a reputation. Everyone.

Knowing that, you might want to be more careful before putting anything in the digital sphere. What you post, even in a personal message to someone else, can be shared. Once you put it out there digitally, it's no longer yours to control.

Alan adds a well-meaning adage, "Nothing is private anymore. Even if it's a private message between two parties on WhatsApp, your friend could easily take it and forward it to someone else."

I next ask Alan about principles that would help young adults in their career journey. "Recognise that employers are checking whatever you post online. Often the test before you post something is, 'Would you be okay if this was a note on your grandmother's fridge?'"

We laugh. It's a good point. In the world of social media today, anything you post has potential ramifications, even if you did not intend it.

Alan's second advice is to grow one's reputation.

"Develop your network. Ensure that within your industry, people are talking about you in a good way, even when you're not there."

The third principle Alan shares is having a reputation of reliability. In today's fast-moving world, it can be easy to make empty promises, and not keep them.

"I will share with you one advice that a famous journalist once told me. He said to me, 'Never miss a deadline, and never waste a word.'"

The idea of reputation, and your reputation in the industry you're in, may be something you've never thought of. But if you're eager to progress, you need to enlist others in doing the work of recommending you to their friends. Cold-calling, and applying for a job online, may work, but it's not the best way.

There are better ways, such as referrals.

There are two reasons why referrals work. Firstly, there is an element of trust between the asker (the employer) and the friend. You will be surprised at how many jobs are filled that way.

The second reason why having a great reputation works is because of how it would seem less like you're boasting about yourself and what you do. But others are instead singing your praises, about how you're doing a great job. This builds your credibility, rather than making you look like a snake-oil salesman.

That starts with having a great reputation in your current work, where you say what you do and do what you say. That's an important principle.

Say what you do.

Do what you say.

It first involves us communicating clearly what we are doing in our work, so that your bosses know what you're doing. Then it involves you delivering on what you say. This reputation for reliability is vital in becoming outstanding in your career.

In Elena L. Botelho and Kim R. Powell's study of 2,600 leaders, they found that the overlapping characteristic determining those who eventually became CEOs was …

Try guessing.

Look at the likes of former Apple CEO, Steve Jobs. Might it be creativity? Or the likes of former US President, Barack Obama. Charisma?

No. The one factor that consistently predicted who became CEOs, and who did not—*reliability*.

They delivered what they said they would deliver, at the quality expected, at the deadline negotiated. Having this dependability and trustworthiness means that others can depend on you to deliver the goods. They can lean on you like an immovable rock. There's nothing more important in the world of business than being able to deliver, when asked to deliver. It's why we are so excited when we see a famous basketball superstar entrusted to take a three-point shot with three seconds on the clock, and like clockwork, he scores.

Imagine if you could have that degree of dependability. You would be the Most Valuable Player of your company.

AFTERWORD

Go to any shelf in the library and you will see hundreds of books telling you how to write a CV, get a job, interview, or find your passion. This book doesn't try to be like those.

We don't want it to be.

When we went through the process of finding the stories to fit into this book, we initially thought we *should* find distinguished luminaries. After all, if you want career success, it makes sense to learn from the best.

But we realised that by doing that, we would miss out on the flip side of careers. Where people fail. Where people go through long periods in the wilderness, wondering what they are doing in their lives. Where people see careers as a trudge, rather than a transformation.

That is the reality of careers for many people. Gallup's 2017 survey of 195,600 American employees found that 16% were actively disengaged at work, miserable, and actively destroying what others were building; 51% were not engaged—they are just there.

Why does work have to be so frustrating for people?

Throughout this book, we have sought to answer that question. We have sought out the places where Gen Zs are flourishing at work, and asked: Why are they doing so well? What about the workplace is contributing so much to their sense of satisfaction with work?

Then we've sought people who've succeeded in their careers. These span the gamut of people from different industries and people at different life stages.

But more importantly, we've sought the people who we would traditionally label as "failures". Because we believe that's the ultimate highlight of grit—crafting success from failure—which will bring you from stage to stage in your career.

Thus, this book is also filled with people you normally would not expect—stories of people who have experienced failure, who might make you go, *I don't want to be like him.*

It's these stories which we hope will inspire you as you read these pages. We hope those stories make you cry, because they made me cry. Whenever I read the story of Ariel, I cry. Only because I know that it wasn't fair how she was treated, and yet this continues unabated, across industries.

This is a book about realities. About the reality that confronts us each and every day when we go to work. Whether we want to put in our best, or give a half-assed standard. Whether we choose to give it our all, or do the bare minimum to survive and collect your pay cheque at the end of the month.

And this book is dedicated to those who, day after day, still punch in, bringing their dreams to work, and hoping for some way to live out those dreams at work. It's dedicated to you who, each day, put your dream in the hands of your employer and ask, "Will you play me? Will you trust me? Will you dream with me?"

Keep dreaming. Keep those dreams alive. Because the future belongs to those who dare, and those who dream.

It belongs to those who grit their teeth through their dreams.

Whatever it takes.

ACKNOWLEDGEMENTS

The reason this book is in your hands, and not in the bin, is testament to the team at Candid Creation Publishing, especially Kok Hwa, my publisher, and Patricia, my editor. There were many times when I opened this manuscript and wanted to trash it. But they saw something in this book that I didn't see. Thank *you* for bringing this to life.

To Jonah, you probably don't remember the conversation we had at Clementi. But there, you told me how it was *okay* to do badly at my A Levels and that you didn't mind having my grades. That was the first time anyone told me that. Throughout these years, you've been an inspiration, helping me to believe, when no one else did.

Kwan, thank you for taking those calls when I ranted. Through those three years in the wilderness, you never gave up on me.

Quek, you too, may not remember the Tampines bus interchange, but it was there that you told me that feeling deeply was not a curse, but a gift. It was then that I began to embrace the gift of my emotions, rather than wanting desperately to be rid of them.

Opal, you spent so many nights (just) to listen to me, which I'm not sure was really the best use of your rest! But without you, I would have struggled to make it through the return to Singapore alive.

And lastly, to our team at Gutenhag—Ling, Steph, Nicholas, Agabus, Jason—thank you for being such a family. Your dreams keep me dreaming.

BIBLIOGRAPHY

This contains a list of resources that I've found most helpful in my journey. I've added a brief sentence for each to share what I think may be most helpful to you.

Brown, Brené. *Dare to Lead: Brave Work. Tough Conversations. Whole Hearts*. London: Vermilion, 2018.
This is a vital book for those looking to understand why we don't live up to our leadership potential, looking at issues that we don't consider much, such as vulnerability in leadership.

Dalio, Ray. *Principles: Life and Work*. New York: Simon & Schuster, 2017.
My favourite book for understanding big picture ideas about life and work. Very deep, and definitely not for the faint-hearted.

Jorgensen, Eric. *The Almanack of Naval Ravikant: A Guide to Wealth and Happiness*. Magarethea Publishing, 2020.

Kaufman, Peter D. *Poor Charlie's Almanack: The Wit and Wisdom of Charles T. Munger*. Marceline, MO: 2005.

Miller, Donald. *Business Made Simple: 60 Days to Master Leadership, Sales, Marketing, Execution, Management, Personal Productivity and More.* London: HarperCollins, 2021.
For those with an entrepreneurial mindset, this gives you the basic skills of building and understanding a business.

Tulgan, Bruce. *Not Everyone Gets a Trophy: How to Manage the Millennials.* Hoboken, NJ: Wiley, 2018.

Tulgan, Bruce. *The Art of Being Indispensable at Work: Win Influence, Beat Overcommitment, and Get the Right Things Done.* Boston, MA: Harvard Business Review Press, 2020.

Tulgan, Bruce. *Bridging the Soft Skills Gap: How to Teach the Missing Basics to Today's Young Talent.* Hoboken, NJ: Wiley, 2015.

Wong, Daniel. *The Happy Student: 5 Steps to Academic Fulfillment and Success.* Singapore: Write Editions, 2013.
For those looking to excel in university, this book offers a framework to make student life more fulfilling.